Assessment in Action

Just-in-time feedback to clarify goals, make progress visible, uncover misunderstandings, and move student learning forward

Theresa Meikle

Pembroke Publishers Limited

538 Hood Road
Markham, Ontario, Canada L3R 3K9
www.pembrokepublishers.com

Library and Archives Canada Cataloguing in Publication

Title: Assessment in action : just-in-time feedback to clarify goals, make progress visible, uncover misunderstandings, and move student learning forward / Theresa Meikle.

Names: Meikle, Theresa, author.

Description: Includes bibliographical references and index.

Identifiers: Canadiana (print) 20240420284 | Canadiana (ebook) 20240420314 | ISBN 9781551383705 (softcover) | ISBN 9781551389707 (PDF)

Subjects: LCSH: Observation (Educational method) | LCSH: Learning—Evaluation.

Classification: LCC LB1731.6 .M45 2024 | DDC 370.71/1—dc23

Editor: Kat Mototsune
Cover Design: John Zehethofer
Typesetting: Jay Tee Graphics Ltd.

Printed and bound in Canada
9 8 7 6 5 4 3 2 1

Contents

Preface

It is my hope that this book will provide teachers with a variety of tools for creating a rich and connected community of learners who support and encourage each other to grow every day. An important underpinning of the book is the recognition of how our "presence" as teachers and students influences one another.

Are we, as teachers and students, fully present in the classroom? Are we socially, emotionally, and cognitively engaged in being together to learn and contribute, to make meaning of our experiences? Our presence matters; our ability to build relationships with our students and to help them build respectful, inclusive, and compassionate connections ripples out into the world. I hope the approaches and strategies here support this desire to build independence and interdependence in and beyond the classroom.

I offer this beautiful reflection from Richard Wagamese to keep before us as we recognize how essential we are to one another.

> "We approach our lives on different trajectories,
> each of us spinning in our own separate, shining orbits.
> What gives this life its resonance is when those trajectories cross
> and we become engaged with each other, for as long or as fleetingly as we do.
> There's a shared energy then, and it can feel as though the whole universe is in the process of coming together.
> I live for those times.
> No one is truly ever 'just passing through'.
> Every encounter has within it the power of enchantment, if we're willing to look for it."
>
> — Richard Wagamese, *Embers: One Ojibway's Meditations* (2016)

Acknowledgments

I'm grateful to all my family, students, teachers, and colleagues, who have helped me continue to grow during the course of my long career in education. It has been by turns rewarding and challenging, exhilarating and exhausting; it has never been dull. I'm indebted to Cathy Costello, who encouraged me to step out of my own classroom to learn with teacher colleagues in York Region District School Board.

This central role provided me with incredible opportunities to learn from and with inspiring, committed, and visionary leaders in education through the Literacy Collaborative, lead by Lyn Sharratt and Beate Planche. In particular, being on a team with Laura Leesti and Candice Mott was a great privilege; here I learned to practice listening, perspective-takinggratitude. Wonderful study tours to the UK with colleagues Kim Smith, Clayton La Touche, Aldrin Fernando, Janani Pathy, Kathy Witherow, and Dean Bodkin were an incredible opportunity to visit classrooms, learn from international educational leaders, and broaden my understanding of the power of assessment to support all learners and to create inclusive, equitable classrooms. This is what it means to learn in community; this is what authentic, deep learning looks like in action. I hope this work has captured this learning journey in a helpful and encouraging way.

Thank you to the teachers and students who shared their thoughts and work samples here: Anna Rebelo, Laura Sermet-Deboer, Stacie Oliver, and Aviva Dunsiger. Thanks also to Noa Daniels and Joanna Thompson-Anselm for our ongoing conversations on all things teaching and learning.

A very special thank you to Jen Giffen for her creation of images of the Habits of Mind, adapted from the work of Costa and Kallick.

This book is dedicated to all my students over the years! They are my most influential teachers. Thanks especially to my most recent students—teacher candidates—at Niagara University in Ontario. They gave me feedback to help me shape this book! I hope it captures a vision for compassionate and equitable classrooms.

Introduction

Every student enters our classroom with their own sense of identity, their own gifts and talents, hopes and aspirations. They also bring their challenges and anxieties. As a teacher, you welcome every student with the intention of helping each one reach their potential. This calls for the development of a caring and respectful classroom climate and positive teacher–student relationships. It develops through the skillful decisions you make, moment to moment and day to day. The timely use of assessment information is key to teacher decision-making and student success. In the past, schools used assessment primarily to sort and rank students. A key practice was summative assessment at the end of a period of study. Student work was graded, averaged with other summative grades, and then reported to the school and guardians. Under these circumstances, students received some feedback—sometimes both grades and comments. Unfortunately, by the time this information was received by the student, the time for the student to act on the feedback had long passed. We moved on to new content and the entire cycle began again, perhaps in a new grade or a new school, but the opportunity to learn and improve learning in a particular area of study was lost. Strategies for assessment *for* and *as* learning shift the focus from sorting and grading students to improving student learning in the midst of the learning.

When you gather evidence of learning during the learning, through observations, conversations, and products, you are in a position to plan effectively to boost student performance. And when students become active participants in the assessment process, they learn to monitor and document their own learning journey. This metacognitive practice builds student autonomy and motivation. The clarity of learning goals and success criteria preview the journey for students and they set goals to make progress.

The curriculum we are required to deliver is a starting point for our planning. We must have a clear sense of what students are expected to know, understand, and be able to do at a particular grade level. We are also tasked with understanding the importance of the transferable and learning skills students need to become global citizens, able to make meaningful use of their learning in the world. These essential skills are cultivated over time and integrated into the curriculum through the processes we use, the products we create, and the collaborative experiences we design for our community of learners. All of this necessitates skillful, integrative program planning. In addition, our plans must be flexible enough to ensure that we are responsive to the student needs we have identified through gathering evidence of learning. Our assessment practices are central to our intention to meet students where they are, engage them in the curriculum, and support them in their academic and personal growth.

Have you ever felt that the expectation to do it all was too much? I know I have. Especially as a new teacher, I felt that getting through the lesson—covering the material, reading the book, assigning the task—were the most important parts of my job. I felt driven to do it all and to make sure my students didn't fall behind. It took me quite some time to see that this was just coverage, rather than deep learning, and to see that my role should be more as a guide and coach rather than a transmitter of information. Although we are expected to have expertise in curriculum planning, subject knowledge, technology integration, social-emotional learning, and effective and equitable assessment practices, we are primarily responsible for knowing who our students are and knowing where each is on their own unique learning journey. When we take deliberate action to build a positive climate for learning, we create the weather of the classroom alongside our students. We are intentional in our approach to relationship-building, collaboration, self-regulation, and the selection of instructional and assessment practices. As teachers, we engage in purposeful planning that seeks to include every student in mindful learning and also anticipates possible barriers to student engagement and progress. We use the planning frameworks of universal design and differentiated instruction to broaden accessibility and to provide appropriate scaffolding. This proactive approach to planning for student success is an essential action that removes obstacles, making classrooms inclusive and equitable.

Cultivating the conditions for student growth does not just depend on us; we build a community of learners in our classrooms and support students in the development of their skills as self- and peer-assessors. You know from your own direct experience that students cannot learn effectively when they do not feel welcomed and cared for—by their teacher and their peers—in their classroom. We all need to feel safe and connected, and to have a sense that we matter to others in our community. Unfortunately, many students do not experience this sense of belonging. When you are explicit in your intention to build student confidence and resilience, you help students develop a sense of agency and to see that they can have a positive impact on others in their lives. They begin to see themselves as contributors, as key members in the classroom community. You weave together the explicit curriculum of academic expectations and the foundational curriculum of mental health and well-being as you build this learning community with your students. This evolving sense of interdependence is built as students become involved in making meaning together. They learn to become architects of their own learning and contributors to the learning of others. Unfortunately, sometimes in our rush to "cover" curriculum, we can forget that teaching and learning come through interaction and relationship. However, we can choose to cultivate the conditions for each student to thrive academically, socially, and emotionally in our classrooms. When we are intentional in our teaching practice, we help students become partners in learning.

Creating a positive classroom community that enables every student to flourish starts with us. We need a repertoire of strategies and practices; we need to select from that repertoire with care and to adapt to the specific context and group of students. This can be overwhelming if we are not clear about our intentions or the learning destination. It can be especially challenging when we are trying to support autonomy, as moving away from teacher-directed, curriculum-driven coverage can feel a bit chaotic. But when you are clear in your intention to support student growth, to develop transferable skills and social-emotional capacities, you can be confident that your skillful and flexible planning will build a strong and connected community.

How to Use this Book

Research over the past 25 years points to the power of effective assessment practices as a key element of student success. This book offers a repertoire of active assessment and instructional teaching practices that help teachers use assessment information to move students forward in their learning. As well, it provides specific approaches to help teachers create the conditions for students to build supportive and productive relationships with their peers. Authentic membership in the learning community also emboldens students to take risks, act on feedback, and improve their academic performance. These practices are part of deliberate backward-design planning for safe, inclusive learning environments in schools. Students become self-regulating, life-long learners with a strong sense of independence and a respect for the interdependence that arises from deep learning in a community of learners.

This book provides techniques and strategies to help shift the balance from a focus on evaluation and grading to assessment that maximizes learning and supports student success. As you know, learning is not straightforward: we begin, pause, take a few steps back, reconsider, adjust, and try things out to see how they fit with what we already believe and do. So this book offers you quotations as Prompts for Reflection at the beginning of each chapter and Learning Journal questions at the end, to help you consider how to use the ideas in your teaching practice. In addition, there are Pause and Ponder points for further reflection embedded throughout the book to enhance your engagement with the ideas and strategies. All these items are included as boxed text. I encourage you to engage in this learning with others and to test it out.

Part A: Building a Learning Community

Chapter 1: Cultivating A Learning Culture

This chapter offers practices for bringing students together in a respectful, responsible, and accountable way.

Chapter 2: Equitable Assessment

This chapter provides research on the importance of identity-affirming and culturally responsive classrooms, and of essential planning considerations, including Universal Design and Differentiated Instruction.

Chapter 3: Planning for Success

This is a review of Backward Design (Understanding by Design), a framework for identifying big ideas, enduring understandings, and assessment tasks that will provide evidence of learning aligned with learning goals and success criteria.

Chapter 4: Navigating, Communicating, and Documenting the Learning Journey

Practices here focus on metacognition, monitoring progress, and making thinking audible and visible through conversation, observation, and products.

Part B: To Sit Beside: The Meaning and Practice of Assessment

Chapter 5: Assessment For Learning: Diagnostic and Formative Practices

Here we explore how we gather evidence of learning and use it in a timely fashion to differentiate instruction and adapt our planning to support further learning.

Chapter 6: Assessment For Learning: Feedback for Growth

Deepening our understanding of student-involved assessment and effective use of success criteria to improve learning

Chapter 7: Assessment As Learning: Self-Monitoring, Revising, and Intentional Practice

Returning to metacognition as a key learning skill and motivator for students.

Suggested Approach

- **Before reading**, take time to consider the prompts and essential questions at the beginning of each chapter. You might choose to annotate the text, write in a journal, or talk them over with a colleague. Consider using the Circle of Viewpoints thinking routine to actively engage with the content. This is an effective practice for activating what we already know and connecting what we know to what is offered in the chapter; it is also effective in prompting us to consider the ideas from a variety of perspectives.

Circle of Viewpoints

1. Consider several viewpoints from which to explore the prompt and/or essential questions (For example: how might a parent, student, administrator, teacher see this idea/answer this question?)
2. Choose one perspective to explore and use one of these sentence-starters:

   As a student I think …
   A question I have as a teacher is …
   An idea that resonates with me as a parent/guardian is …

- **As you read**, consider what elements of these practices you already have in place. How might you add to or refine them?
- **After you read**, take note of what practices you currently have in place that you might let go of to make space for what is new and promising.

PART A

Building a Learning Community

In 1968, Paulo Friere pointed out that students are often positioned as passive recipients of information. He termed this as a *banking model* of education. This concept regards students as banks into which teachers make "deposits." Friere argued that this model of education sees students as objects, rather than as human beings with potential, promise, and agency. This approach cultivates passivity, rather than inquiry and engagement. When I started teaching, I did not intentionally choose such an approach in my classroom, but there were certainly elements of the banking model in play, as I often made all the decisions about what was to be learned, how it was to be learned, and the time allotted to the learning. We certainly play a very important part in planning the learning journey, but it is not straightforward route. Our students are unique and the dynamic in every classroom is created by the individuals in it. Part of my learning journey has been toward a more student-focused approach. When we use information to inform next steps in learning, we are responding to the human beings in front of us and differentiating our instruction based on where each is at the moment.

The four chapters that follow will focus on how to build community and help students see themselves as active participants in the learning process rather than mere recipients. The strategies and suggestions offered will support the development of a classroom culture that welcomes and honors every student, and is responsive to their identities, strengths, interests, and areas for growth. There is an important focus on academic content and the importance of student belonging, connection, and equity.

CHAPTER 1

Cultivating a Learning Culture

Prompt for Reflection

> "It is worth noting right from the start, that assessment is a human process, conducted by and with human beings, and subject inevitably to the frailties of human judgment. However crisp and objective we might try to make it, and however neatly quantifiable may be our 'results', assessment is closer to an art than a science. It is, after all, an exercise in human communication."
> — Sutton (1991)

- What aspects of this observation ring true in your classroom experience?
- What factors make this challenging? How have you already found ways to address the challenges?

Essential Questions

- What conditions foster learning and engagement?
- How does assessment empower learning?

This chapter offers practices for bringing students together to form a respectful, responsible, and productive learning community. Each year or semester, we bring together students with diverse abilities, interests, experiences, and identities to learn a common curriculum. As noted by Ruth Sutton (1991), and observed by many others, learning, teaching, and assessing are human processes that involve constant social interactions. You move through the day making observations, asking questions, gathering information, listening to responses, and responding in the moment to provide feedback and direction. You are constantly in motion as a teacher—cognitively, physically, emotionally, and socially. Our students are also constantly in the midst of these interactions, and each interaction affects the one that follows. These relational dynamics can be positive, energizing, and productive to our learning, and they can also be negative, draining, and disruptive of the learning. Co-constructing classroom norms and returning to them regularly supports the development of a positive and engaged learning community.

Co-Constructing Norms

Co-constructing norms with students models a collaborative approach for students and helps them understand their personal, social, and working responsibilities. It also helps us share the responsibility for the learning culture of the classroom with students; it develops student identities as active partners in learning. Teacher and students create the climate of the classroom together.

Co-constructing norms can be done in a variety of ways, simple and complex. Depending on the age of your students, you might choose to provide them with a number of examples of norms and the vocabulary they will need to select or determine what will best work for them as effective group members.

Strategy: Constructing Norms Together

- Pose these questions to the class:

  What do we need to keep in mind when we are working together?
  How do we think it should feel, sound, and look like if we are working well?

- Allow students an opportunity to offer their answers to the whole class and record on the whiteboard.

Feels Like	Sounds like	Looks like
• fun • friendly • nice	• talking • inside voices	• sitting with friends • sharing stuff and ideas

- Now have students work with a partner to flesh out the list, perhaps on a whiteboard; encourage them to be specific and add details. Perhaps provide a sample list of norms and adjectives from which they can select, based on what they think is most important.
- As a whole class, cluster and categorize the norms students have suggested and make a manageable list that everyone understands. Tease out any that are unclear to get at what students really feel is important to working and learning well together.
- Draw attention to norms that were well-managed; perhaps identify a norm that might have been overlooked to focus on the next day.

Note: It is essential that this is seen as a work in progress. Students can refer to it at the beginning of a lesson and select one that they will really focus on that will help them on that particular day. You can also have students return to the norms through the day to reflect on whether or not they are maintaining them, individually and as a group, and what might need to be done to adjust their approach. This is a form of metacognition, as students plan a particular approach or way of being that will enhance their learning and social skills. It is also a way to model monitoring progress and making adjustments to meet goals. It lays the groundwork for meaningful assessment for learning practices and as learning practices.

Sample Chart of Group Norms

Our Group Norms	
Be Kind • listen to other people • take turns speaking • speak with a soft voice • share the pen/marker • include and encourage everyone	Be On Task • focus on the learning goal/task • ask questions • add ideas • keep trying

The Role of the Teacher in an Assessment-Focused Classroom

You have many roles to play in your classroom and each class of students requires you to adjust, adapt, and respond to the learners you have before you. Some students will look to you for confirmation that they are on the right track by constantly seeking affirmation, while others will work away with confidence that they are moving forward. Some might try to stay under the radar, hoping that you do not know that they are lost or struggling. Take a moment to think about when an assessment a student submitted was a surprise to you. It might have been better than you expected or it might have been far off target. Either way, it is information for you to use and an opportunity for you to provide feedback. Sadly, this information often comes to us too late to act on. If we are constantly eliciting information from our students about their learning, we might still be surprised, but we will know early enough to support our students through reteaching, providing scaffolded feedback, or prompting them with an effective question to probe their thinking.

How can you support each student in a way that builds their confidence, empowers them to work independently, and ensures their progress? Building assessment-for-learning and assessment-as-learning practices into daily instruction supports this intention.

We are in meaningful dialogue with students about the learning, their developing understanding, and ways we can adjust our approach to respond in the midst of the learning. This is a constructivist approach that centres the student as an active, capable, and competent learner. As their teacher, you still have an essential role in the classroom, but the emphasis shifts from the teacher as the keeper of knowledge, and positions students as co-learners in community.

Teacher Presence

Presence refers to our self-awareness, awareness of others, and awareness of context in the moment. It includes awareness of our feelings, actions, gestures, and interactions with others while they are happening. It also involves awareness of the ever-changing dynamics of the classroom; it is an ongoing exercise in communication, curiosity, and collaboration. It views teaching "as engaging in an authentic relationship with students where teachers know and respond with intelligence and compassion to students and their learning" (Rodgers & Raider-Roth, 2006). The relationships we build in our classrooms are essential to student success. Students look to us for information about whether we care for them and respect them as individuals. Students wish to be seen and valued by us and by their peers. We let them know, through our authentic presence, if we care for them as individuals and if we know where they are as learners. Only by being immersed and attuned in the learning community with our students can we connect and respond with the clear intention of supporting their growth, both academically and in the development of social-emotional skills.

We communicate our presence through our tone of voice, body language, gestures, facial expressions, posture, etc., and so do our students. Students are constantly taking cues from one another, and from us, about how things are progressing in their learning and whether or not it is safe to take a risk by asking a question or offering an answer. Developing our own self-awareness and becoming critically reflective practitioners helps us learn and develop our presence. Students are constantly communicating with us; when we are present, we are attuned to their experiences and have an opportunity to respond to them in a skillful and timely way.

Being compassionately and skillfully responsive to all that is taking place in the classroom is challenging. It requires agility and adapting in the moment. And it requires a strong sense of stability, a repertoire of effective strategies, and a clear sense of purpose. When we are able to adapt to student needs from a place of grounded awareness, we are practicing *with-it-ness*. Hattie (2012) refers to this as a "certain mindfulness… about what is happening and what is likely to happen that can affect the flow of learning for each student" (p. 69).

This table is adapted from Andrew Markelz (ASCD), where he summarizes some key "with-it-ness" practices—Engage, Scan, Praise (ESP)—as helpful strategies to practice this responsiveness.

Engage	Scan the Classroom	Praise Growth
• interact with students constantly to reduce drifting, distraction, and boredom • redirect to learning goals, success criteria, and self-regulated learning	• observe the interactions and support healthy relationships • circulate amongst pairs and groups • annotate observations • pose a question • remind students of expectations for collaboration and team-building	• reinforce desired actions, attitudes, and collaboration • classroom norms are invaluable here, especially if they have been co-constructed • point out what is working well and redirect, with kindness, as necessary

Finally, it is through our classroom presence that we model for students how to handle their emotions, both pleasant and unpleasant. When we respond to inappropriate student behavior in a confident and caring way that resolves conflict, we are showing students how to do the same. We model for students how to develop and maintain healthy relationships through our attentive listening, caring responses, genuine interest, and focused attention. The development of social-emotional skills is a lifelong pursuit and these skills are taught both explicitly and implicitly. Identifying and managing emotions, stress management, perseverance, and motivation are cultivated over time, and are essential to our well-being and sense of belonging in the world. They are foundational to our academic achievement. A classroom that builds in assessment for learning and assessment as learning as a daily practice also cultivates these essential life skills. Teacher actions include

- teaching students metacognition explicitly and embedding reflection and timely feedback during the learning
- teaching the language of assessment to students and guardians
- engaging students in conversations about their learning and thinking
- co-constructing success criteria and discussing exemplars
- modeling for students how to provide effective feedback to peers, based on success criteria and exemplars
- supporting students in the development of healthy, respectful relationships, in which all voices are valued and encouraged
- providing opportunities to practice and debrief assessment conversations
- providing students with many opportunities to seek out, value, and act on feedback from peers
- engaging in self-reflection to sharpen our awareness of our values, beliefs, and biases
- viewing student learning and performance as feedback about our instructional decisions and adjusting instruction appropriately

The Role of Students in an Assessment-Focused Classroom

Students are active participants in their learning and are motivated co-learners in the community. They develop their social-emotional capacities through interaction with others, and see that they can make significant contributions to the community. They start to see themselves as contributors: capable and competent learners. In addition, they come to see the value in learning alongside others, even those they might have ignored or excluded in the past. As we build community together in the classroom, students develop a stronger sense of belonging and mattering.

Strategy: Daily Greetings

"Students benefit from knowing that they matter to an adult, as well as to their peers. Encouraging students to develop relationships with both staff and students will set them on the path of increased connectedness at school and create opportunities for learning and skill development."
— School Mental Health Ontario

The purpose of this strategy is to acknowledge and welcome students, and show them that they are valued, to celebrate diversity, and uniqueness; and to model the importance of taking time for relationship-building at school

1. Greet students each day as they come into the school/class and during transitions. Greetings can include
   - Greeting students by name and/or in their first language
   - Saying "hello" in a different language every week and having everyone join in
   - Asking students about something in their day
2. Apply the 5 × 10 rule:

   If someone is within 5 feet/1.5 m, say hi!
   If someone is within 10 feet/3 m, make eye contact and smile.
3. Encourage students to use the practice throughout their own day.

Student actions include

- understanding where they are going and what the learning destination looks like
- articulating what success looks like and identifying elements in their work that meet the success criteria, noticing what is missing and what requires refinement
- planning, monitoring, and adjusting approach based on peer, teacher, and self-assessment
- building relationships with other learners and encouraging contributions of others
- supporting others on the learning journey
- taking an interest in the work of others
- demonstrating curiosity
- identifying what meets success criteria and why
- posing questions for others to consider
- offering constructive feedback
- suggesting next steps
- soliciting and considering feedback from others and determining how to use it to move forward

Learning Skills
- **Self-Regulation**
- **Initiative**
- **Responsibility**
- **Collaboration**
- **Organization**
- **Independent Work**

Creating the conditions for students to become learning resources for one another and to take responsibility for their own learning is essential. These conditions are initiated through the explicit instruction from teachers; however, they are maintained and grow through the relationships developed in the classroom. When we are deliberate in building the learning skills into our planning, we are supporting students to develop independence and interdependence.

Metacognition

Metacognition is at the heart of learning. It helps students develop a sense of agency and self-efficacy, and it underpins the learning skills we need to be successful and engaged learners. It has a number of components, identified through the research of Flavell (1976) and developed through the work of many researchers.

Metacognitive awareness is the conscious aspect of thinking about our thinking; metacognitive strategy is the employment of what we learn through this process. Metacognitive awareness helps us self-regulate, take responsibility, and motivate ourselves to keep going, while metacognitive strategy helps us plan how we approach a task, monitor how well we are doing in accomplishing the task, and evaluating how effective we have been in completing the task. This can be very challenging if students do not feel comfortable asking for help or taking risks in the classroom. Students are supported in becoming active learners when they feel a sense of connection to the other learners and their teacher. Part of this has to do with being aware of their feelings in the midst of their learning and actively choosing to encourage themselves and others through positive interactions and self-talk. We build a sense of community through engagement in the learning and through the skillful processes of productive talk. There are a number of practical strategies we can use to support the development of listening, speaking, and knowledge-building skills, such as providing time for thinking and allowing processing opportunities with peers.

Metacognition enhances our ability to complete work independently, organize our approach in terms of resources and time management, and collaborate with others effectively. Coordinating all of these demands of the classroom requires deliberate attention and reflection. Think–Pair–Share and Say Something reading are valuable strategies for developing metacognition and building community.

Strategy: Think–Pair–Share

The purpose of this strategy is to provide students with an opportunity to think about a question or prompt from the teacher on their own. It can also be used before or after engaging in a task to reflect on how well students understand what they are doing and to consider what might help them make progress.

- Individually: Students think, then write a short response to a prompt.
- Pair: Students take turns sharing and listening to one another's answers.
- Whole-class Share: Call on students randomly to share something from their conversation. In this way, students are accountable to the learning and also supported, because they have had time to think on their own and learn from a peer. After hearing from a number of students, you can then clarify, address misconceptions, add to ideas, or summarize for the class.
- You might choose to bring two partnerships together to combine their answers as a group of four and ask them to summarize their response and share it on chart paper or the board. This helps students make learning visible and document the learning journey. The class can return to these answers as understanding develops over the course of the unit.

"Teachers who help students develop and internalize metacognitive strategies through direct instruction, modeling and practice promote learning because the effective use of such strategies is one of the primary differences between more and less able learners."
— Jay McTighe (Wiggins & McTighe,2005)

Tips

- It is key that think time is actually practiced. We often rush through this part of the strategy and lose the benefit of the individual's time. This strategy is an excellent way to allow students who require a bit more time to think through an idea, and it prevents more confident students from rushing in to provide a ready answer. It is a simple and manageable way to support those who need extra time and those who are capable and ready to develop a more detailed response.
- Providing students with a journal, notebook, or organizer to record thinking moments is also helpful for students to track their thinking and to summarize conversation in a visible way. This can also be done through the use of digital tools, such as whiteboard, slide show, etc.

These teacher samples are variations of think–pair–share. Notice how the effective use of technology supports student collaboration, builds knowledge, and makes thinking visible. This is a powerful tool for students to document their learning and hold on to thinking during the learning process.—Samples reproduced with permission of Laura S-D.

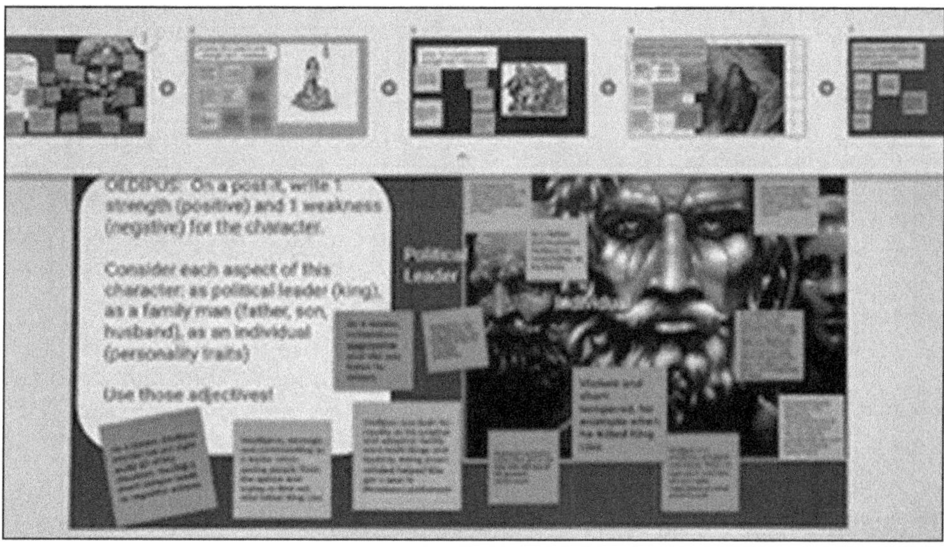

Strategy: Say Something/Draw Something/Write Something

This strategy provides stem starters to scaffold student engagement and comprehension with texts. It can be used with fiction, nonfiction, print, digital, or multimodal texts. It can be done through conversation, illustration, and/or writing.

1. Students are assigned to read the same text, aloud or silently. Then, at predetermined stopping points, they take turns making connections, making a comment, asking questions, clarifying, etc. The following prompts are samples and can be adapted to meet a specific text form.

Partners can be assigned randomly or intentionally for this strategy. It depends on the purpose of the task and the grade level.

Make a connection
- *This reminds me of...*
- *This setting/character/part is like...*

Make a comment
- *I like how the writer describes...*
- *This makes me wonder because...*

Ask a question
- *What do you think the writer means when they say...?*
- *A question I have about this is ...*

Clarify
- *I think this part means..., but I'm confused about...*
- *This part is important because...*

2. After using the strategy, debrief with students. What did they find helpful? Challenging? How might they use the strategy differently next time? How does talking about what they are reading help them think differently? What perspective or information did their partner bring to the conversation that changed their thinking? How might they use this when reading independently? This metacognitive reflection helps students understand that learning is an active process of meaning-making, and that, when they stop to check their understanding, they become more skillful and active learners.

Strategy: Entry and Exit Tickets

Entry and exit tickets are excellent supports to build metacognitive habits of mind, and they are excellent assessment-for- and assessment-as-learning tools. They help you know which students are on track and which students need additional support. They are also helpful for students, because they help them identify and explain what they know before class begins, and support them in consolidating what they have learned at the end of class. See ticket templates on page 22.

See page 22 for templates.

You might choose to collect all of the tickets or just select four or five students randomly to have a sense of where they are. All students can keep a record of these cards to track and document their progress.

Exit/entry tickets can also be used to help students practice giving quick feedback on a short task. The success criteria below can be used to help students provide feedback and/or can be a starting point for students to co-construct success criteria for more detailed entry/exit tickets. This will help students understand the purpose and value of feedback as a support for their growth and learning, not for grading.

Entry Ticket Success Criteria	Exit Ticket Success Criteria
• focuses on the prompt • provides specific detail • supported by an example	• answers the question directly • provides relevant information • shows understanding of ideas and vocabulary

Learning Journal: The 3 Whys

1. Why might this topic matter to me?
2. Why might this topic matter to the people close to me, personally and professionally?
3. Why might this topic matter beyond my context, out in the world?

Entry/Exit Tickets

Identify and explain the most important idea you remember from last class. What helped you remember this idea?	Identify what learning skill you have been developing and explain how you used it today.

Write a headline to summarize the main concepts from last class.	Explain how your ideas about ____________________ has changed during this unit.

Pembroke Publishers ©2024 *Assessment in Action* by Theresa Meikle ISBN 978-1-55138-370-5

CHAPTER 2

Equitable Assessment

Prompt for Reflection

> "Each educational space conveys a story about safety and belonging. Students learn whether their identity matters through curriculum, the pedagogical approaches or dispositions of educators, policies, peer interactions, and features within a physical environment. The classroom can be a place that nurtures intellectual capacity, promotes joy, and fosters a sense of community. However, the classroom can also reflect oppressive systems and practices that hinder learning experiences and dehumanize the identities of learners. As custodians of space, our beliefs about children and their histories are a critical factor in the creation of an identity affirming environment."
>
> — Buchanan-Rivera (2022), *Identity Affirming Classrooms: Spaces that Center Humanity*

- Consider this quotation in light of the learning spaces in your school.
- What stories do those spaces—classrooms, library, offices—tell about your beliefs about your community and your learners? Are these "spaces of possibility"?

Essential Question

How can our assessment practices create an equitable and inclusive learning community?

Every student has the right to develop their full potential, and schools are critical in this journey. How can we create the conditions for every student to see that there is space and time for them in our learning environment? In this chapter, we will consider what gets in the way of learning and offer specific approaches that can lead to engaged, and even joyful, learning.

Our schools are diverse communities and, as such, can encompass many dimensions and interactions in identity, such as physical abilities, race, ethnicity, gender, sexual orientation, socio-economic status, age, spiritual and political beliefs, etc. We are also diverse in terms of ability, personality, interest, talents, etc. Equity in assessment meets individual needs, identifies and eliminates obstacles to learning, promotes a sense of belonging, and involves the broader community in the learning journey. Our assessment practices have a key role to play in identifying and supporting the unique needs of every learner, in making learning accessible and engaging, in building an interdependent learning community in which every student has a felt sense of safety and belief in their own value and identity. In addition, our partners in education—i.e., guardians, parents—also see themselves and their identities reflected in our assessment and instructional decisions.

School Mental Health Ontario provides many resources to help us address the issues of inequity in our schools. They provide equity-focused strategies to help us address the range of barriers students experience in school and beyond. We can improve equity in our schools by noticing, naming, and addressing inequities in the experiences and outcomes for all students and adults, and cultivating identity-affirming environments across race, gender identity, ethnicity, language, disability, sexual orientation, family background, family income, and other characteristics.

> "Equity commitments are vital in addressing the unfair distribution of access and opportunities resulting in disparities that are based on identity markers like race, gender identity and expression, sexual orientation, religion, ethnicity, culture, immigration status, first language, ability, etc." (School Mental Health Ontario)

There are many ways to support students in recognizing their own gifts and valuing the gifts of others. Selecting texts that meet our learning goals and our overarching equity goals is key to building an inclusive environment and supporting students as they see themselves represented.

In his book *The Gift of Story: Exploring the Affective Side of the Reading Life*, John Schu cites a beautiful journal by Dr. DasGupta that speaks to the heart of this idea:

> "Health, in its fullest definition, is a sense of wholeness—an ability to move through this world knowing you and yours are loved, valued, and celebrated. Librarians (not to mention teachers, coaches, neighbors, friends—anyone who has the opportunity to share stories and celebrate reading with young people) are then also in the business of health. Stocking, reading, sharing, recommending, and celebrating stories in which all our children can see themselves are practices of healing, a way to write a healthier future for our world into being." (Schu, 2022, p. 17)

Schu goes on to share books that show us what it means to be compassionate, to connect with ourselves and others, to be inspired and to inspire, to clarify our understanding, and to heal.

Pause and Ponder

- How have stories helped you do all these things? As a child? As an adult? Which ones come to mind for you?
- How have you seen this work in your classroom? What stories have helped students show compassion to classmates? What stories have provided comfort and healing?
- What stories have really resonated with your students, helping them see themselves and also to value diversity?

Strategy: Positive Affirmations

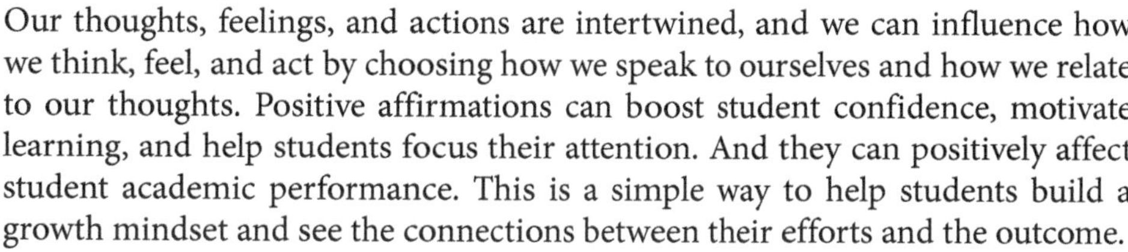

Our thoughts, feelings, and actions are intertwined, and we can influence how we think, feel, and act by choosing how we speak to ourselves and how we relate to our thoughts. Positive affirmations can boost student confidence, motivate learning, and help students focus their attention. And they can positively affect student academic performance. This is a simple way to help students build a growth mindset and see the connections between their efforts and the outcome.

This strategy will be useful for all students at the beginning of the school year and could become more important to their progress when they start to experience a challenge that seems hard to move through. You might choose to post positive affirmations in the classroom as shared affirmations, or students can have their own affirmations in their desk or in a journal. The strategy can be incorporated into Language Arts, Art, and Social Studies lessons, as students explore heroic characters and see that everyone has challenges and yet we can all persist—especially when things are hard.

1. Talk to students about the importance of trying hard and talking to themselves, and each other, in a positive way.
2. Consider sharing the books *Trying* by Kobi Yamada and/or *Big* by Vashti Harrison to help students understand what it means to be courageous, confident, and kind to themselves.
3. Read through some examples of positive affirmations and have students start to create their own.

I am becoming a strong reader.
I was a kind friend today.
Math is fun.
I'm proud of my spelling work.
I pay attention and get my work done.
I will try it again.
My work is getting better.
I'm on the road to improving my art.

Strategy: My Marvelous Moment

Recognizing our successes and being able to attribute them to our efforts helps us become strategic learners. This strategy can be used at the end of a lesson, unit, or evaluation period.

1. Have students reflect on their progress and notice something they accomplished that they initially found really challenging.

2. Use prompts to help them identify what specific strategies or learning skills they used to help them through the learning.

   What was the hardest part of this for you?
   What helped you get better at it?
   How do you think you could use that skill again in the future?

Pause and Ponder

- Think back to your experiences as a student, at any age, and take a few minutes to recall an incident in which you felt affirmed, seen, and valued as a contributing member of your learning community. What led to those feelings?
- Now, think about another moment, perhaps a more difficult one, that left you feeling embarrassed, insecure, or even shamed. What led to those feelings?
- Keep these reflections in mind as you consider some of the actions teachers and a community learners can take in order to experience more of the affirmation that comes from learning and to ease the stress of the inevitable challenges.

You might have witnessed fellow students, colleagues, or young people you care for struggling in a new learning experience. This is expected, and some discomfort, or productive struggle, can certainly help us stretch and grow; however, when the learning goal is cloudy or too far from our reach, we can become so discouraged that we give up. If this is a child's daily experience as a student, if learning is constantly a struggle and they feel they are out of step, lagging behind, they might start to get in their own way by engaging in unproductive behavior—avoidance, acting out, tuning out, etc. They might also start to feed into the idea that they are not good students and engage in self-talk that makes them feel even worse. This might lead to school induced anxiety and eventually school avoidance.

Bring to mind a situation in which you were treated unfairly as a result of who you are. What was the impact of that treatment on you—in the moment and thereafter?

> "The child started reading and everything went along fine until she got to that word. It was only five letters, but there might as well have been twenty there. She said it the way her father had told her, but she knew it was wrong, because Miss Choi would not turn the page. Instead, she pointed to the word and tapped the page as if by doing so the correct sound would spill out. But the child didn't know how to pronounce it. Tap. Tap. Tap.
> Finally, a yellow-haired girl in the class called out, "It's a knife! The k is silent," and rolled her eyes as if there was nothing easier in the world to know."
>
> —from *How to Pronounce Knife* by Souvankham Thammavongsa

Pause and Ponder

- How does this situation connect to your own experience as a student? parent? teacher?
- How might this experience shape the child's next moments and days at school?
- How might we approach it differently from an assessment equity lens?

I share this story because when I read it, it reminded me of my own embarrassment reading aloud in class as a newcomer to Canada. English is my first language and I was a fluent reader; however, my Scottish accent got in the way. I felt like an outsider and I was constantly reminded of my difference. Although this classroom moment was not a deliberate attempt to embarrass me, it did. My confidence was shaken. I tried to adopt a Canadian accent, very quickly, to blend in. I couldn't get some of the words right, right away—"book" had a long "oo" sound for me! As the youngest of seven, I was the only one of my family to try to eradicate my accent. It was odd; I spoke with a Canadian accent at school and a Scottish accent at home. I just wanted to belong. This seemed the fastest way to escape notice, to disappear. You might be reminded of one of your students who feels they must relinquish part of their identity to fit in. This comes at a cost, as Brené Brown reminds us through her work with Grade 8 students who generated the following distinction between true belonging and fitting in:

> "*Belonging* is being accepted for you. *Fitting in* is being accepted for being like everyone else." (Brown. 2015)

Identity-affirming classrooms value students as unique, worthy, and capable.

When you consider your own experiences and these stories, you might observe that the hurt that came out of these moments was not a matter of a teacher or community intentionally trying to shame anyone, but the impact remains the same—a sense of feeling an outsider or "less than" for the student. We have the tools to change this classroom dynamic when we approach our work through an equity lens. We can welcome newcomers, and everyone else, with an appreciation that we are all unique, worthy of respect and capable of meeting high expectations.

Welcoming Students

Some approaches can help our newcomer students begin to adjust and to feel welcome in our classrooms, and are helpful supports for all of our students:

- create time to build a welcoming community within the classroom that helps students include and welcome newcomers
- meet and greet students each morning and take time to connect with them
- support classroom routines with visual reminders
- design the classroom space to reflect the diversity of the students and community
- encourage use of first language and translanguaging, allowing students to use their "linguistic repertoire in a fluid and dynamic way, mixing and meshing languages to communicate, interact, and connect with peers and teachers" (Planning for English Language Learners, Ontario Curriculum and Resources).

Strategy: Mix and Mingle/Connecting with Images

Combining these two strategies builds community and student engagement as students interact with each other in a light-hearted and curious conversation. This can be built into a lesson on effective listening and speaking, or it can be done as a transition activity to introduce a new topic and generate excitement and connection.

1. Choose a selection of images. Images can be chosen intentionally to focus on a thematic unit or they can be selected at random. They should be appropriate for the age group and representative of the students in the classroom. This strategy is appropriate in any grade.
2. Provide students with a series of simple images and have each select one to which they can make a personal connection. The connection might be to a feeling, a memory, a story, etc.
3. Once students have selected their image, they move around the room to a piece of music. When the music stops, they find a partner and take turns sharing and listening to each other.
4. Keep this short and warm-hearted, light.
5. Ask students to share a connection and perhaps note how an image can be interpreted in a variety of ways. This will help them consider other perspectives.
6. Provide an opportunity for students to debrief the strategy. What was helpful? What was challenging? This can be done together or silently in a journal, to provide a little privacy.

Universal Design and Differentiated Instruction: Frameworks for Planning

When we are intentional in our approach to planning, so that all students have equity of access to the curriculum through universal design for learning and differentiated instruction, we help students thrive. You might have observed that many of your learners engage in writing tasks that are clearly structured and allow them to choose from a range of digital tools to craft a response. Other students take longer to get started and could benefit from the support of conversation, partner work, illustrations, sentence starters, and graphic organizers to get on their way. When we provide options for everyone in our classroom, we are removing barriers and enabling access for all. This benefits everyone, as students are given choice and support they can choose to use to meet their learning goals. This is the Universal Design approach that has come to us through the design principles of architecture—making access to buildings easier for everyone, using such structures as ramps and stairs. This approach makes buildings —and learning—more invitational and approachable for everyone. It offers choice and recognizes that we are unique; we are uniquely talented, able, and resourceful. This planning principle helps teachers encourage and accommodate all students. Key features of Universal Design for Learning (UdL) include flexibility, inclusion, multimodality, and choice.

Differentiated Instruction (DI) is an important partner to Universal Design, as it provides the additional support of precision and customization to meet students' specific interests, talents, and difficulties. So, UdL opens the door and DI provides additional options and a variety of targeted supports. We can differentiate in the moment, as we engage in conversations with students during class and listen in to students' conversations. This provides us with the opportunity to provide just-in-time feedback.

The combination of both of these frameworks ensures that everyone is provided access to the learning and that the learning is targeted and responsive to where students are in their learning journey.

The following classroom practices can help us think about how to incorporate UdL and DI into our everyday planning:

Adapted from *Learning for All* (Ontario 2022)

- ensure that the classroom is a caring and supportive learning space where everyone is included and each student's contribution matters
- ensure students understand what they are learning while they are in the midst of the task; this distinction helps them see that the focus needs to be on mindful learning, not just going through the motions, and gets at the *why* of the task
- help students see what the learning goal looks like and see that it is within their reach; provide examples, anchor charts, etc.
- plan instructional and learning strategies that are flexible and varied
- offer multiple entry points and provide opportunities to extend learning for all students
- organize the use of space to minimize distractions and offer choice
- employ a multimodal approach; make use of all the senses and different types of texts (print, online, audible, visual, etc.)
- make varied use of space and groupings; pairs, triads, small groups
- offer multimodal means of presenting/creating their work
- uncover misconceptions in the moment by listening closely to students and observing them as they work and provide just-in-time feedback to move students forward
- provide ongoing assessment and adjust instruction in response to assessment information
- ensure access to various types of information and digital tools to facilitate learning
- document and respond to evidence of student learning (observations, conversations, and products)
- engage in professional inquiry that focuses on the process of students' learning

Culturally Responsive and Relevant Pedagogy

In *The Courage to Teach,* Parker J. Palmer suggests that "we teach who we are," that we cannot separate our pedagogy from who we are as individuals. Our work is always informed by what we value as individuals. Another key insight from Palmer is that "teaching is a daily act of vulnerability." We can feel especially vulnerable as teachers as we try out new practices and feel unsure about how they will land in our classroom. Our students also feel this vulnerability as they navigate learning, their emotions, and their social interactions in the midst of it all. The classroom is a dynamic space of growth and possibility. Developing our self-awareness and identity, and supporting students in doing the same, is important and foundational work in establishing an inclusive and equitable learning community. A great first step is taking the time to look at our own identities.

"Being responsive to diverse students' needs asks teachers to be mindful and present. That requires reflection. Engaging in reflection helps culturally responsive teachers recognize the beliefs, behaviors, and practices that get in the way of their ability to respond constructively and positively to students. ... This means we each must do the "inside-out" work required: developing the right mindset, engaging in self-reflection, checking our implicit biases, practicing social-emotional awareness, and holding an inquiry stance regarding the impact of our interactions on students."
— Hammond (2015)

This activity can help us discern our social location.

This resource on cultural humility can help us reflect on our own beliefs, values, and biases. https://smho-smso.ca/online-resources/cultural-humility-self-reflection-tool-for-school-staff/

Teacher Strategy: Identity Mapping

1. Locate an image that represents something about your identity. It could represent family, interests, cultural background, aspirations—it is up to you! This can also be done just with words: lyrics, quotations, etc.
2. Start to add additional images or words that represent some aspect of who you are.
3. Write a brief description of yourself based on your map. Who is this person? Are all aspects of your identity revealed here? Are there some parts of yourself you don't wish to share with others or even with yourself?
4. Set it aside for a while and come back in a few days to consider what you might add or remove.
5. Share your identity map with a trusted friend and ask them if there is anything missing that the friend sees in you.
6. Consider how your identity intersects with your students' identities. How might your perspective influence your instructional and assessment decisions? What perspectives might you have overlooked? What professional learning can help you broaden your perspective and/or examine your bias?

Strategy: Identity Mapping

The Identity Mapping teacher strategy above can be adapted for use with your students:

1. Locate an image that represents something about your identity. It could represent family, interests, cultural background, aspirations—it is up to you! This can also be done just with words: lyrics, quotations, etc.
2. Start to add additional images or words that represent some aspect of who you are.
3. Write a brief description of yourself based on your map. Who is this person? Are all aspects of your identity revealed here? Are there some parts of yourself you don't wish to share with others or even with yourself?
4. Set it aside for a while and come back in a few days to consider what you might add or remove.
5. Share your identity map with a friend and ask them if there is anything missing that the friend sees in you.

Tips for Implementation

- It can be simplified for any grade.
- It's a little bit like Show and Tell.
- It can be a very helpful in getting to know your students, helping students build connections with one another, and creating a sense of community.
- Depending on the grade level and maturity of your students, you may decide to layer the strategy by having students create identity maps of characters in the stories they are reading or in the online games they like to play.
- You can add vocabulary of character traits to support students' thinking and language acquisition.
- You might share the identity maps on the classroom walls to look for connections and also what makes each of us unique.
- You might choose to share the book *My Map Book* by Sara Fanelli and have students create heart maps.

See https://youtu.be/D9lhs241zeg?si=Wu07JmZZv_adK9Bw

- You might share the video *The Danger of A Single Story* by Chimamanda Ngozi Adichie with older students; this could lead to learning about perspective and voice and bias.
- A more complex version of the strategy is to have your students create a Social Location reflection. This can be a multimodal creation or just plain text.

These samples were created by teacher candidates with a particular focus on their social location and literacy background. Permission to share samples has been granted.

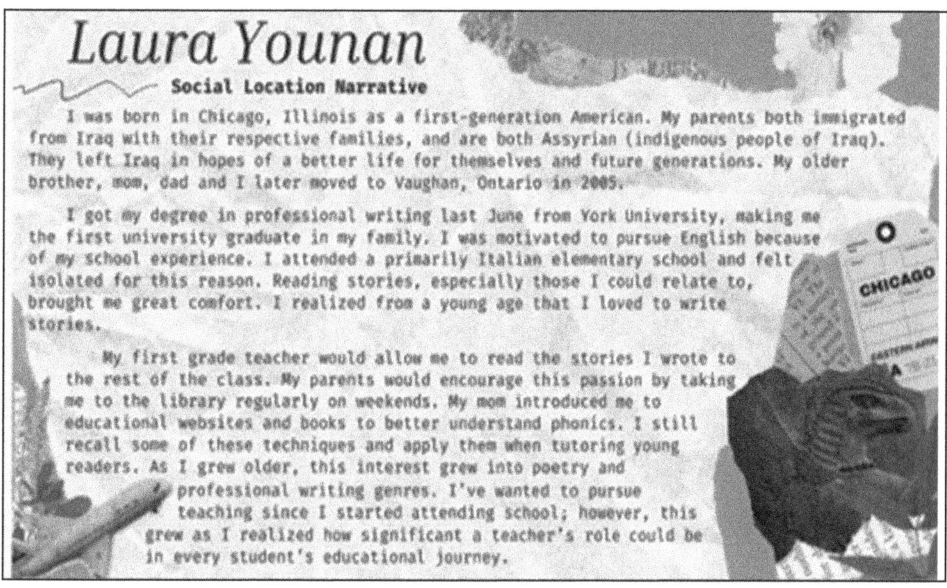

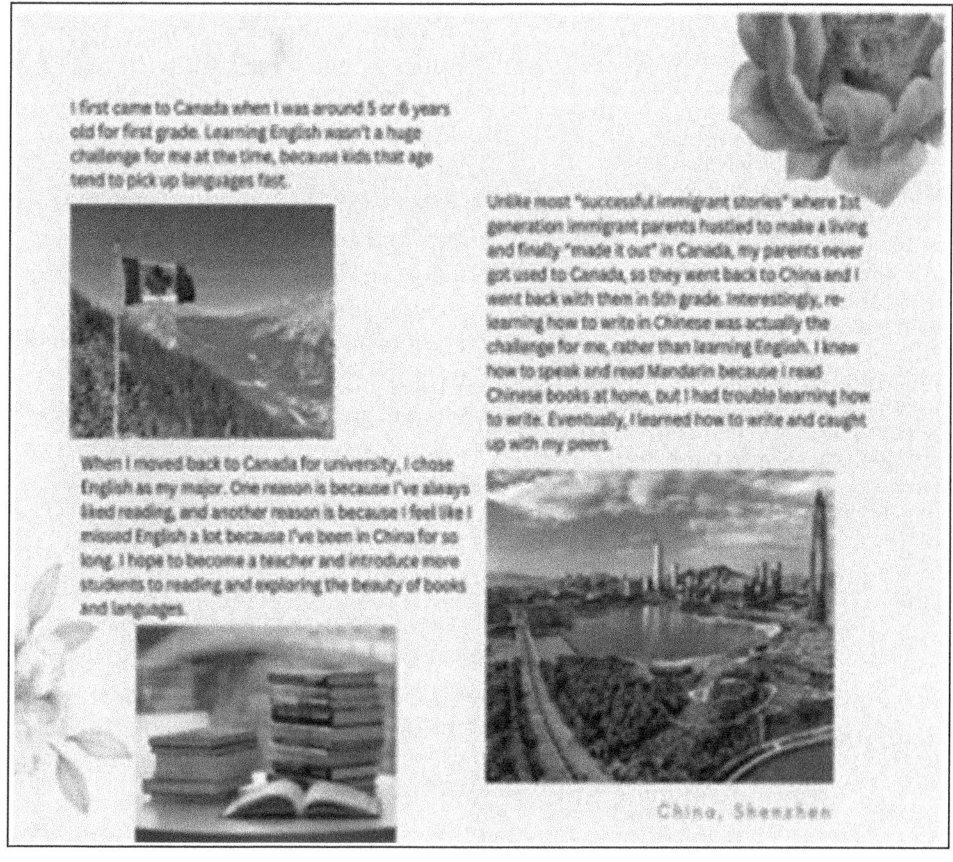

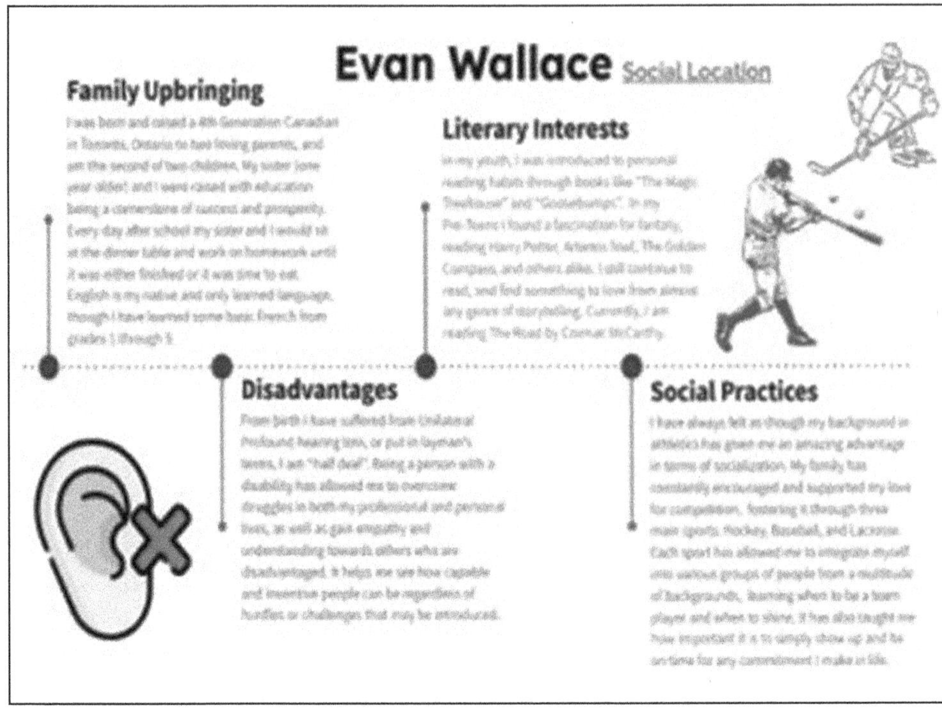

Tips for Making Assessment Equitable for All Students

"If you are teaching a lesson plan or a unit plan, I want you to ask yourself, How is this learning helping my students learn something about themselves, others? What skills am I teaching? Intellect, what new knowledge am I teaching about people, places, communities, and the world? Critically, is my lesson plan or unit helping students become woke to understand oppression, race, racism, sexism, ableism, classism, equity, power, representation, exploitation?… And joy, how am I elevating beauty in humanity? We need joy, you all, now more than ever."
— Muhammad (2023)

1. Plan assessments prior to planning instruction. (More on this in Chapter 3)
2. Ensure students understand the learning goal.
3. Co-construct success criteria, if possible, using examples at a variety of levels.
4. Keep learning goals and success criteria visible and accessible for all.
5. Scaffold the learning with many opportunities for teacher modeling, individual and collaborative practice.
6. Support students with many opportunities for reflection through self- and peer assessment.
7. Design tasks that have multiple entry points, using a Universal Design for Learning approach.
8. Use multiple kinds of assessments to gather evidence of the full range of student learning: open response, formative quizzes, anticipation guides, graphic organizers, thinking routines, such as I Used to Think: Now I Think, Four C's, Headline Summaries, entry and exit tickets, conferences.
9. Provide reasonable timelines and deadlines.
10. Check for progress and provide feedback or reteach as necessary.
11. Ensure your materials are accessible for everyone: consider language, text, visuals, digital tools; i.e., all available supports.
12. Come back to examples regularly.
13. If possible, engage in assessing student work with colleagues to calibrate understanding of learning goals and to plan next steps in instruction and for student feedback.
14. Provide options. Although students are working toward learning goals that are derived from the curriculum, the route to meeting that destination can include choice. That is, students may choose to represent their learning in a variety of formats:

- visual presentations
- speeches
- essays
- presentations
- videos
- dramatizations
- podcasts

Learning Journal: Step In, Step Out, Step Back

- Take a moment here to skim over the chapter and reread sections that were of particular interest.
- Step In: What does this chapter ask you to consider about the purpose(s) of education and the role of teachers?
- Step Out: What would you like to learn to understand and actualize the ideas in this chapter more fully?
- Step Back: What do you notice about your own perspective and experiences with regards to the ideas advanced in this chapter?

CHAPTER 3

Planning for Success

Prompt for Reflection

"Understanding requires knowledge, but goes beyond it. Understanding depends on richly integrated and connected knowledge. This means that understanding goes beyond merely possessing a set of skills or a collection of facts in isolation; rather understanding requires that our knowledge be woven together in a way that connects one idea to another. This web of connection and relations becomes the vehicle for putting our ideas to work and seeing the applicability of our skills in novel circumstances and in the creation of new ideas."

— Ritchhart (2015)

- How does this definition of understanding fit with your experience as an educator? As a student?
- What experiences have led you to deep understanding?
- How might these ideas about understanding inform your instructional and assessment planning?

Essential Questions

- How do we identify the big ideas (core concepts) in the content standards?
- How do we ensure that what we are measuring is meaningful, relevant, and transferable to other contexts?
- What does it mean to really learn and understand something?

There is too much to do as a teacher. You have many decisions to make about what to include in your lessons, what to give most time to, and how to make the most of the limited amount of time you have with your students. Sometimes the content standards can feel like an unwieldy obstacle rather than a helpful guide on the learning journey. As teachers, we are committed to helping students learn and grow, but sometimes we are not sure what they are supposed to learn or how to track that they are on the right road.

Backward Design

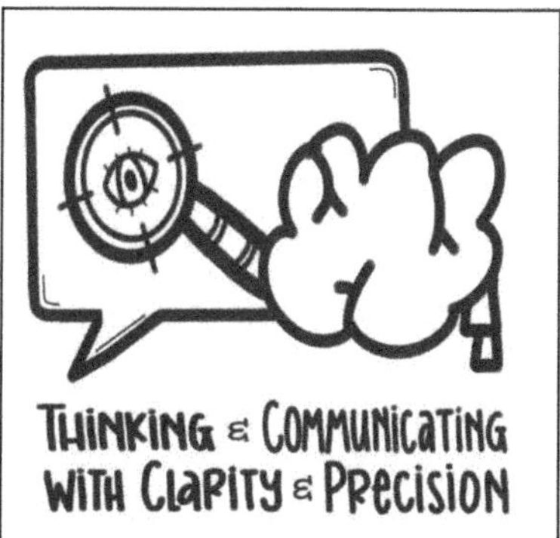

The Understanding by Design framework, often called Backward Design, developed by Wiggins and McTighe in 1998, provides us with a practical structure to make decisions and prioritize what matters most in learning. In addition, it helps us align our instruction and our assessment with our learning goals from the outset. We begin with a clear vision of the learning destination and plan accordingly. We also ensure that the learning is meaningful, relevant, and "sticky"; that is, students retain and use what they have learned in real-world contexts.

You may already be very familiar with this model, or something similar. The key idea is that, as instructional and assessment designers, we understand that we must begin with the end in mind. We are clear about what is important to learn and we also have a strong sense of what types of evidence will help us track whether or not students are making progress.

The clarity and precision that can arise out of this planning approach can reduce our sense that there is too much to do and move us to a place of enthusiasm for the journey ahead. As a beginning teacher, I did not have this sense of clarity. I was very fortunate to have generous colleagues who shared many resources with me—many, many binders filled with tasks, questions, and sequences of things to do. As I reflect on this, I realize that this was helpful, but in some ways it contributed to the sense of being overwhelmed. How would I ever do all of these things? Which ones were most important to do? Backward Design can help you determine this in a three-step process:

Step 1: Identify where we are going; this is the learning destination. This is derived from the content standards as you unpack and cluster them to determine the big ideas and skills that students are to develop. This step is critical in helping identify what is most important for students to learn. It helps us focus your efforts and your assessment/instructional practices.

Step 2: Select relevant assessment evidence and design the culminating task that students are working toward. Ensure that the task matches the kinds of learning goals you are assessing in the unit.

Step 3: Design the learning plan; this includes the learning activities and builds in space for many assessments for/as learning opportunities.

Notice that this type of planning focuses on the alignment of the learning goals with assessment and instruction. Rather than choosing activities first, we choose the learning activities that are most likely to engage students in the learning that we intend, and we help them navigate the journey through clarity about success criteria and quality performance.

Adapted from *Understanding by Design* by Wiggins and McTighe (2005)

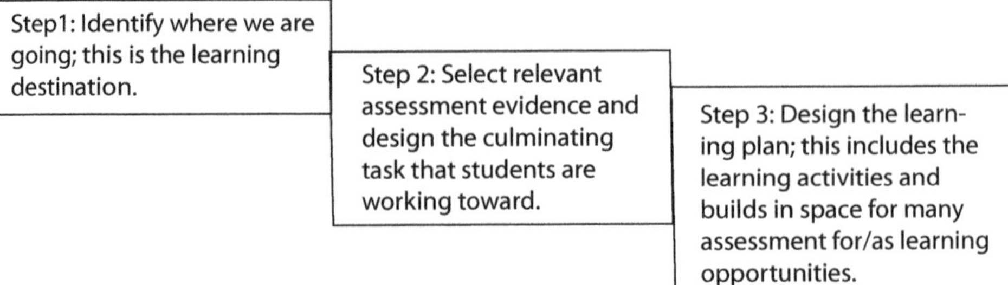

Step 1: The Learning Destination

In this step we identify the core concepts, principles, theories, and processes the content standards require. These big ideas are transferable beyond the scope of the course; they are applicable in familiar and new situations. Big ideas help us link discrete facts or skills in a coherent framework. When we plan from the beginning with the big ideas we want our students to really invest in, we address two challenging issues in our classrooms: the problem of *aimless coverage*, or delivering content without making meaning of it; and the problem of *isolated activities* that keep students busy, but do not necessarily lead to learning.

This stage also asks us to formulate questions to drive inquiry, and foster understanding and transfer of learning. These are our essential questions from page 34. The graphic on page 38 helps us understand this process of identifying what matters most for student learning. All learning goals are not equal, and we have a responsibility to identify what is most meaningful, relevant, and empowering for the students we have before us.

Step 2: The Assessment Evidence

Identifying the big ideas helps us then ask these questions: *What evidence can I gather that will show what students know and can do? What are the best assessment methods available to me to gather relevant evidence and respond during the learning?* There are many ways to gather evidence; however, the point here is to ensure that we are actually measuring what we intended students to learn. This requires that we make connections between the learning goals and the assessment tasks that we design. What are we looking for in the student work? Are we measuring what we intended to measure? Are we measuring what is meaningful, relevant, and valuable for our students to know, understand, and be able to do now and in the future? Effective planning helps us create a coherent and meaningful program that results in authentic learning.

Step 3: The Learning Plan

In this step we design the learning experiences and instruction that will enable students to achieve the desired results (the learning goals and big ideas). We also know what observations, conversations, and products we might employ to gather evidence about progress on the journey.

When I was a fairly new teacher, this approach to planning helped me prioritize, plan, teach, and assess with greater confidence. I moved from seeing my role in the classroom from being primarily an activity designer to becoming an *assessor*—a critical distinction.

Take a moment to read the following chart and consider the questions. Do you think primarily like an assessor or an activity designer? Both are important. Which comes first for you?

Inspired by *Understanding by Design* by Wiggins and McTighe (2005)

Planning and Thinking Like an Assessor	Planning and Thinking Like an Activity Designer
• What information will I gather to show that students really understand the learning goals during the learning? • How much evidence will I need to consider it valid and reliable? • How will I track student progress? • How will students be involved in tracking their own progress? • What incremental tasks will both build and reveal understanding? • What culminating tasks will we build toward? • What kinds of learning goals am I assessing? Knowledge/Understanding? Reasoning/Thinking? Skill/Product? • Which kinds of assessment tasks best match the learning goals I'm assessing? • Am I clear about the success criteria and levels of quality that will demonstrate mastery? • How will I help my students understand what quality looks like? What examples or mentor texts can help us understand what quality looks like? • How will I build in time for feedback—teacher, peer, and self—during the learning? During the Unit • How is it going? • What might I need to adjust? At the End of the Unit • Where are my students now? • What might I need to revisit before moving along?	• What resources and units are ready to go on this topic? • What topics and projects will students want to do? • What will be cool and fun for students? • How will I test students? • How will I generate a grade for the work students do or produce? During the Unit • Does everyone have enough to do? • Am I covering the curriculum? At the End of the Unit • How did it go? • Were students busy? • How did students do on the tests? • Did I cover the standards?

Pause and Ponder

What insights or questions do you have based on your reading of this chart? How does this information fit with your current approach? How might it be helpful in streamlining your planning and assessment practice?

We need to be both assessors and activity designers; however, if we are clear in our understanding of the desired results from the outset and we know what evidence we will collect as a culminating task for the unit, then we can design the learning effectively to move students forward. Our work is intentional and focused. Students understand where we are going, know what success looks like, and understand how each step is moving them toward the learning destination.

A reminder here that planning is an iterative process. We make a plan and we continue to revise based on the evidence we gather from our students each day. This is essential in order to be responsive to our students and to ensure each student moves forward.

We do need to select meaningful and engaging activities for students to engage in their learning, but we must always ensure that they serve a clear purpose. There are lots of interesting and fun things to do in school, and it is essential that we consider our students' interests and instructional starting points, but the activities must always be clearly connected to our learning goals. Knowing how we will track growth toward the learning goals from the outset helps us align our activities and our assessments. Students are then engaged in relevant, meaningful tasks that serve both purposes—instruction and assessment for and as learning. This is how we gather evidence and provide just-in-time feedback during the learning.

Culminating tasks anchor the learning in a unit of study. They are multifaceted, providing students with a rich opportunity to show their accumulated knowledge, understanding, and skill over a period of time. Students understand what this type of performance looks like and they develop the skills to create it through the experiences and learning stages of the unit. The activities and feedback are focused, and we avoid the problems of meaningless coverage and irrelevant activities. We are aligned in our learning goals, in our instruction and assessment practices.

You might find it helpful to keep in mind this model as you are planning and responding. Notice that teaching and assessing are happening simultaneously. As we use formative assessment—assessment for and as learning—in the midst of the learning, our instruction and assessment practice is woven together. We are constantly gathering and responding to evidence of student learning through our observations and conversations.

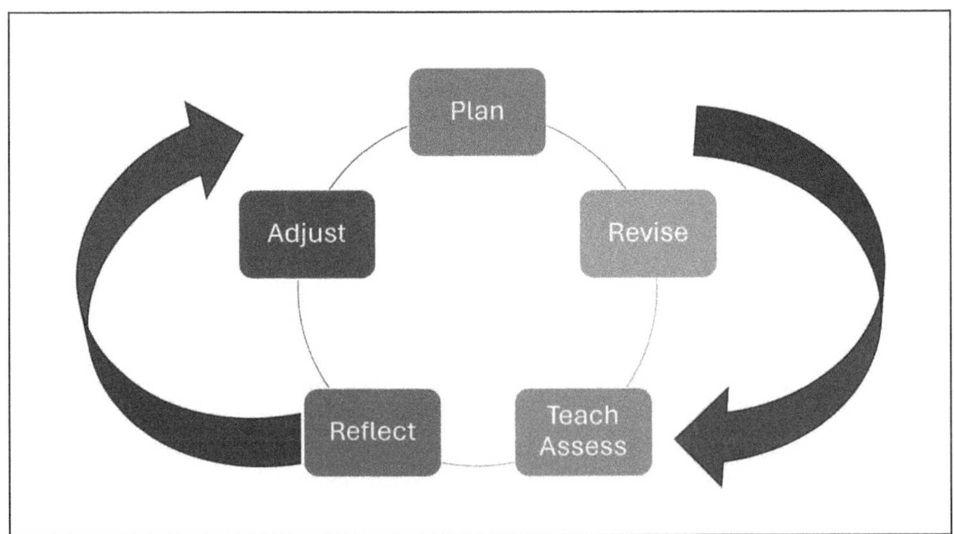

Backward Design helps us think deeply about the big ideas in the content standards and how we will measure student achievement. This is essential, in order to provide meaningful and specific feedback. We need to be clear on what is to be learned and also what success looks like.

All the evidence we gather about student performance generally fits into four areas of learning, within which our learning goals can be organized and measured: Knowledge, Reasoning/Thinking, Skill, and Products. These types of learning-goal categories are interrelated and essential for us to consider as we plan for students to show the full range of their achievement. They move us beyond a focus on knowledge acquisition and guide us to teach and assess students as thinkers, communicators, and global citizens. They help us plan for learning, which enables students to apply and transfer their learning in relevant and authentic context. All four categories are important and essential to the development of an assessment map; this is a clear journey to identify, communicate, document, assess, and support students to make meaningful progress. Note that students are at the centre of this process. Their involvement in assessment is key to their progress and motivation to learn.

Students as Active Agents

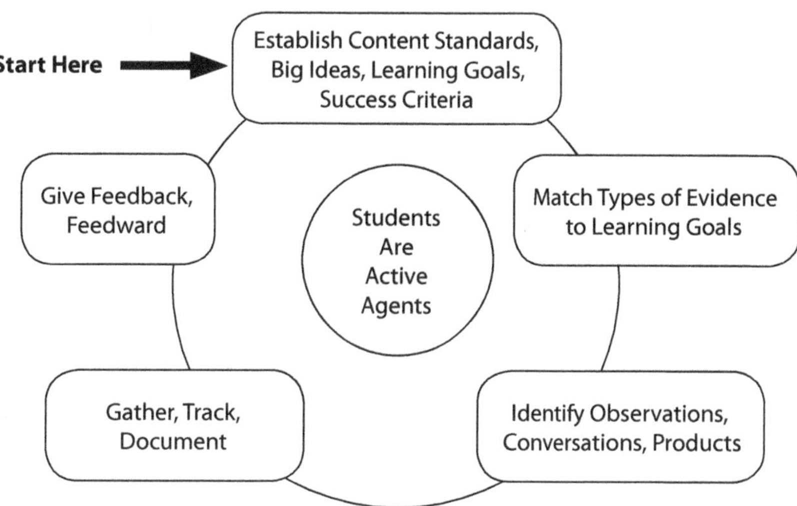

The key is to ensure that the learning goal is clear and consistent. When we assess student learning we ask ourselves, *What does student work reveal about the student's achievement of the learning goal? What does this student know and understand? What skills has this student demonstrated? What are the next steps for this student? What feedback will help the student move forward?*

We need to align our instructional and assessment practices with the learning we are looking to see from our students. Taking the time to understand content standards is key. We notice that the standards call for certain kinds of evidence. Some standards identify learning that is mostly Knowledge; i.e., the subject-matter content that students are to know, facts and/or procedures. In Language Arts that might include some of the following: morphology, text features and text forms, strategies for making meaning, and creating texts. Learning that focuses on Reasoning/Thinking requires students to use critical and creative thinking for a variety of purposes. To demonstrate reasoning, students use knowledge and understanding purposefully to draw conclusions, consider perspectives, pose questions, etc. Skill and Product learning focuses on the communication, application, and transfer of Knowledge and Reasoning. Students have opportunities to be involved in deep learning as they use what they know and understand in novel demonstrations. The chart below summarizes these different types of learning goals.

Types of Learning Goals

Knowledge/Understanding Learning Goals	Reasoning/Thinking Learning Goals	Skill and Product Learning Goals
• subject-specific content • facts • procedures • concepts	• using knowledge and understanding to solve problems, form judgments, draw conclusions • critical and creative thinking	• completing a process • demonstrating an activity • creating a product • communicating and transfering understanding into familiar and new contexts

An additional consideration here, as we embark on our planning, is which type of assessment is best to measure these different aspects of learning. Matching the assessment method, or the task, with the learning goals is key to understanding where students are and to provide them with specific and relevant feedback. This helps us ensure that we are measuring progress and enables us to communicate learning in a valid and reliable way. When we are clear about the nature of the learning goals, we are better equipped to decide what kind of task will elicit the right evidence of learning. The different types of learning targets help us make reasonable inferences and, eventually, judgments about the quality of student learning based on a comprehensive body of evidence gathered over time.

There are many highly valuable and quick ways to measure knowledge targets, such as quizzes, multiple-choice, and true-or-false, and many can take advantage of various technologies. These can yield valuable formative assessment information and should not be overlooked as a source of evidence of student learning. Of course, they can also be used to gather summative assessment information. Here we are concerned with information that can help us before and during the learning, so any of these short response items can be used to enable both students and teacher to see where they are in relation to the learning target. Formative quizzes can advance student learning when students have time to identify where they went wrong and the opportunity to learn from their mistakes. This prevents the scenario of the summative quiz that merely judges learning, rather than enhancing it.

Student self-assessment is a key enabler of academic achievement and motivation. The list of strategies highlights a few that can be incorporated on a regular basis to help students move closer to meeting the success criteria and become metacognitive and self-directed learners. As mentioned earlier, this is a key goal of assessment for and as learning.

The list below offers a classification of assessment methods that can help you consider a variety of ways to gather evidence of learning. All of these methods have their place in the classroom. Although some are less formal than others, each provides powerful evidence of student progress. Observations and Conversations are often seen as separate processes, yet they are often intertwined in the learning process and provide teachers with important information at the moment. The Products are, generally speaking, more long-term, complex demonstrations of learning, used as culminating tasks at the end of a period of learning. They are developed through scaffolded processes and many self-, peer, and teacher assessment reviews prior to any summative submission.

Conversations, Observations, Products, and Student Self-Assessment

Conversations

Quick Check-In Strategies

- thumbs up, down, sideways

- quick sketch
- hashtags
- find the flaw
- Tweet it (280 characters)

Checking for Understanding
- classroom discussion with many students involved—basketball, not ping pong
- assessment conversations with teacher and/or peers
- oral and written feedback
- 2 Stars and a Wish
- index cards
- 3 interesting points/2 wonderings/1 hashtag summary
- analogy prompt
- invent a 3-question quiz with a partner
- graphic organizers
- mind maps

Oral Questioning
- informal to formal
- whole-class
- small-group
- individual
- conferences
- interviews
- role-playing

Observations

During group tasks or evaluating language skills or mathematical concepts, direct observation provides valuable data to inform teaching strategies and lesson planning.

- formal, focused
- examining work in progress
- anecdotal
- noting and providing support in development of learning skills in the moment
- organization
- responsibility
- independent work
- collaboration
- self-regulation
- initiative

Checklists
- recording evidence of success criteria
- met/not yet
- photos and videos of student work and interactions
- direct observation focusing on specific learning goals and success criteria and/or learning skills

Products

The following assessment methods are best suited to eliciting evidence about Reasoning and Skills and Product learning goals:

Paper	Poem	Video/Audio
Project	Portfolio	Spreadsheet

Webpage
Exhibition
Reflection
Journal
Graph
Speech
Presentation
Demonstration
Dramatic Reading
Debate
Recital
Enactment
Sport performance
Dancing
Spoken Word
Podcast
Analytical Essay
Personal Essay
Visual / Verbal Essay
Multimodal Essay
Digital Diary
Manifesto
Table
Illustration
Lab report

Student Self-Assessment

- Attitude survey
- Metacognitive journal
- Success criteria reflection checklist
- Response to feedback
- Portfolio/Documentation
- Stars and Stairs with Evidence
- Student-led conference
- Proof cards
- Goal-setting
- Self-reflections
- Peer assessment
- Reflections on peer feedback

You might recognize many of these strategies as ones you already use purposefully to track and respond to student learning. We will discuss the how, why, and when of these strategies in the upcoming chapters. An important idea to keep in mind is that our assessments can be used for a variety of purposes; however, we decide before we select a particular strategy how the information we elicit about understanding will be used. In this book, we are primarily talking about using strategies to advance learning. When reporting is required, we can consider all the evidence we have gathered to make a professional judgment and provide a snapshot of where each learner is relative to the success criteria. This is criterion-referenced reporting.

Please see the Unit and Lesson Planning tools in the Appendix on pages 117–119.

Learning Journal

As we wrap up this section on planning, let's return to one of our essential questions: *What does it mean to really learn and understand something?*

At the opening of the chapter we reflected on what it means to understand in a deep way. Ritchhart (2023) suggests that it is about the weaving together of connections, one idea to another. The following summary from the work of Ambrose defines learning as a process that is invisible, active, and done by students. Learning leads to understanding and change. "In the context of learning, motivation influences the direction, intensity, persistence and quality of the learning behaviors in which students engage." (Ambrose, Bridges, DiPietro, Lovett, & Norman, 2010)

Learning is a process	Learning is done by students	Learning leads to change
Learning is a process, not a product. It takes place in the mind. We look for evidence of learning through making thinking visible through the processes, performances and products we ask of students.	Learning is not something done to students, but rather something students themselves do. It is the direct result of how students interpret and respond to their experiences—conscious and unconscious, past and present.	Learning changes knowledge, understanding, behaviors, and attitudes. Learning is not fleeting; it has a lasting impact on how we think and act.

Take this moment to reflect on how the planning framework offered here—identifying desired results, determining acceptable evidence, and planning learning experiences and instruction—supports student motivation and leads to learning that is relevant, meaningful, responsive, and transferable. How do the practices here lead to learning and understanding?

Consider completing this 3-2-1 Exit Card to capture your own learning and next steps:

3 New or refreshed ideas in this chapter
2 Practices you want to try out
1 Question you have about implementing an idea

CHAPTER 4

Clarifying, Documenting, and Navigating the Learning Journey

Prompt for Reflection

"For someone to be able to navigate, by land or by sea, they need two pieces of information — where they are and where they are going. Both pieces of information are vital and of equal value. If they don't know where they are going, they are destined to get lost. And if they don't know where they are, well, then they are already lost."
— Liljedahl (2021)

- Have you ever had this experience as a learner? What helped you find your way?
- Take a moment here to identify the strategies you already use to help students know where they are in relation to the learning goals and to support them in developing a clear understanding of where they are going.

Essential Questions

- How do we make the learning destination clear for students?
- How do we involve students in tracking their progress?

The preceding chapter helped us think about how we determine learning goals and decide upon the evidence that will help us know whether or not students are making progress toward them. In this chapter we will consider how we will support students in understanding the learning goals and help them document their progress. We want them to know where they are going and we don't want to lose them on the way.

Our first challenge is ensuring that the language we use to describe the learning destination is clear for students, and for parents and guardians. Since we have already clarified the learning goals for ourselves, perhaps in collaboration with colleagues, we are now ready to consider how to make them accessible and visible for students.

A few considerations here:

- Students: Consider what this group of students needs, as a group and as individuals. What do they already know about learning goals and success criteria? How much experience have they had with this approach? How might you frame this approach in a way that garners interest and motivation?
- Vocabulary: Generally, we want to keep subject-specific terminology in the learning goal, but we also take the time to define it.
- Complexity: Perhaps we need to break down the learning goals we identified into smaller, more digestible chunks.
- Abstract nature of some learning goals: Sharing exemplars—a range of strong and weak—can help students refine their vision and clarify their understanding.
- Context: Helping students connect the new learning goals to what they already know about the content and/or to associated skills they can draw upon can relieve anxiety and help them access the prior knowledge that can support them along the way.

Our work is to help students understand what they are to learn, and to respond to their questions about the learning goals. It is not sufficient to share the learning goals on the board or digitally, and then assume that students understand where they are headed. Examining exemplars together at a variety of levels of proficiency and identifying the characteristics of the exemplars also helps students develop a sense of the success criteria.

Sharing, Clarifying, and Using Learning Goals and Success Criteria

Samples of provocations to start a lesson.

Learning goals need to be clear to the teacher from the outset; however, they do not always need to be shared with students at the beginning of the lesson. Learning goals can be uncovered through inquiry and exploration.

Student engagement is enhanced when lessons start with novelty. You might use as a provocation an image, a short video clip, a question, a ticket in the door, a quick write, a quotation, a partner conversation, etc. Something cognitively and socially engaging that connects to the learning goal and provides some context for the class can build interest and excitement. This can help move learning forward and support students in activating their schema: what they already know and think about a particular idea and the connections they can make between ideas.

For example, an image like the ones on page 45 could invite reflection on a variety of issues: rules and responsibilities, personal freedom and age restrictions, attention, distraction, learning, mental health, and social media. It could then lead into persuasive writing or the development of a multimodal creation to address a social or health issue.

Although we have a clear learning goal in mind, we are always trying to make it relevant and responsive for students. Some students will follow along with a clear sense of purpose; many might struggle to understand, so we might need to recalibrate the goal. If our intention is to bring everyone on the journey, we might need a few detours and rests along the way. This flexibility is key, and reminds us that coverage is not the same as learning. Also, students need time to internalize the goal. Some students might already be there; some might be far from the goal. This is what it means to differentiate instruction. We also differentiate the learning goal. We are all headed in the same direction, but not at the same rate. Flexibility is key, and differentiating in terms of content, process, product, and environment can support all students in moving forward.

A Model of Differentiation

Based on model of Differentiated Instruction in Tomlinson (1999)

Principles of Differentiation
• respectful tasks for every student • flexible groupings for learning (homogeneous, heterogeneous, random) • continuous assessment and adjustment • just-in-time feedback and opportunity to act on it
Methods of Differentiation
• varied content: choice and voice in what is learned/explored • options in terms of how students learn and participate in learning process • alternatives for how students demonstrate their learning (evidence of learning)
Identifying Instructional Starting Points and Monitoring Progress
• Where is the student now? • What is the next step for them toward the learning goal(s)? • What learning skill, habit of mind, and/or social-emotional competency will support them at this point?

Learning goals can unfold through inquiry. As we move further into the learning, we work to make it more concrete and visible for our learners. We can do this in a variety of ways. Simply asking students what they learned that day can be helpful information for us and can allow us to keep on top of misconceptions. Often, when we ask students what they learned, they tell us what they did in class, but they don't always make the connection between the "doing" and the "learning." Students might be focused on task completion—a performance goal—without considering why they are completing the task—the learning goal. We must make the learning explicit by asking the question, "So, as you were working on this problem today, what did you learn?" Students can answer by presenting us with facts they uncovered, skills they were developing, or something they understand more deeply as a result of the activity. The question helps them see their own progress and also notice where they are struggling. This is essential to students developing a sense of agency and self-efficacy.

Students can make a note in a learning journal or document their learning in a digital diary to keep track of their progress and build their understanding.

My Learning Journal	
What did I learn today? What is my evidence? What do I know or understand better? What new skills am I developing?	What was the best mistake I made today?
What was interesting, fun, challenging, surprising in today's learning?	How did my mistake help me learn?

Making Learning Visible

Documenting the journey in the classroom space and online plays a huge role in supporting metacognition.

> "Board and/or wall space for co-constructed documentation, anchor charts, shared writing texts, student-generated inquiry questions, etc. supports this meaning-making process. The classroom walls, and collaborative digital spaces, help students build knowledge collaboratively." (Education Leadership Ontario, 2012)

Teacher sample: math prompts courtesy of Anna R.

Helping Students Explain Their Thinking in Mathematics

Prompts To Use:

I know the answer is ______ because I...

I solved the problem by...

The math strategy I used to solve the problem was...

The steps I followed were...

My strategy was successful because...

Teacher sample: learning goals courtesy of Aviva D.

Teacher sample: learning goals courtesy of Anna R.

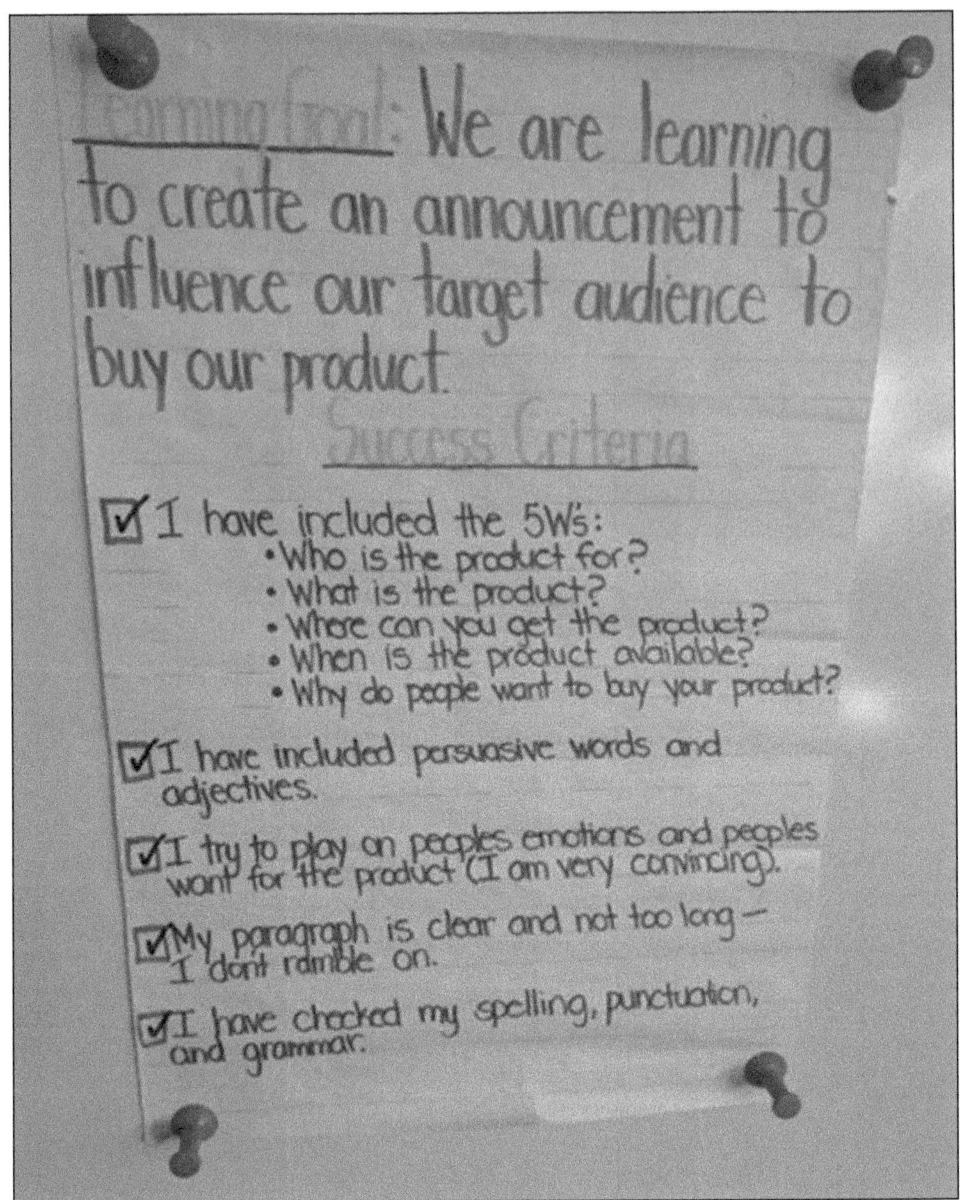

Displaying and referring to visible learning goals and success criteria with supporting samples empowers students as owners of the learning and as self-assessors. As discussed, this is similar to returning to co-constructed classroom norms. When we keep the goals in front of us as visible signposts, we continue to come back to them to see that we are on the correct path. This helps us take stock and re-route if necessary.

Bump-It-Up Walls

Bump-It-Up walls are an excellent visual support to help students define and understand quality. They consist of work samples that show progression in a particular subject area and illustrate the achievement of specific learning goals. They are annotated and reviewed regularly by both teacher and students. Students refer to them to assess their own progress and identify next steps for themselves. These visual reminders keep the success criteria in mind and support learning conversations with students, parents, and colleagues. This is extremely important to help us continue to refine our understanding of the thinking and skills our students are developing, and to pose questions about where we are going next.

Proof Cards

Students can make their learning visible by using Proof Cards to connect their work to the learning goals and success criteria. This helps them document their growth and reflect on next steps. Proof cards prompt students to locate and examine evidence of their learning journey. They then attach that evidence to the card. This can be done in paper or digital form and maintained in portfolios.

Adapted from *Knowing What Counts: Self-Assessment and Goal-Setting, 2nd ed.* by Gregory, Cameron, and Davies (2011).

This shows that …

This part is funny. I made it funny by …

This work is my favorite because …

This was tricky because …

Environmental Nudges

These tools remind students of the destination and support them on the way. They build autonomy and reinforce the active role of students in the assessment process. The Habits of Mind anchor charts provided in the Teacher Tools (pages 122–125) can support students in understanding how to become strategic and capable learners.

Co-Constructing Success Criteria

Co-constructing success criteria takes time and effort. However, it engages students in understanding quality. Students analyze, compare, and contrast to uncover what makes writing effective.

This process is adapted from the work of Sandra Herbst and Anne Davies with a Grade 2 class in *Co-Constructing Success Criteria: Assessment in the Service of Learning* (EdCan Network).

Co-Constructing Success Criteria: Grade 2

1. Teacher shares and reads samples aloud for the class (as appropriate for grade).

2. Teacher poses a question: "Grade 2, what makes this a good piece of writing?"
3. Students talk with a partner and write down one thought.
4. Teacher walks around and listens in.
5. Teacher shares back to whole class what students have noticed in the work.
6. Teacher writes and posts what students say to keep the thinking visible.
7. Teacher adds a few criteria they feel are essential and explains them to students.
8. Teacher shares another sample or two with students and reads them aloud.
9. Students keep looking for evidence of "good writing," and the teacher adds to the shared list the class is developing.
10. Students continue to work with a sample to find evidence of the criteria in the work; they are "connecting to criteria."
11. Teacher Action
    a) Begin to sort the criteria, putting similar ideas together, and then have students contribute to the decisions.
    b) Ask students to suggest a title for each of the groups (classification of criteria).

Co-Constructed Criteria: Draft

Co-Constructed Criteria: Draft
• Category 1: Others can read my writing. • it's neat and we can read it
• Category 2: My writing is interesting to others. • it uses interesting words
• Category 3: My writing follows the rules of writing. • There is a capital and a period.

    c) Provide students with a new sample of writing.
    d) Have students work with a partner to find evidence from each of the three categories in the writing and identify them with different colors:

Category 1: green
Category 2: orange
Category 3: blue

Final Steps

12. Have students exchange papers to check for agreement and build understanding.
13. View the sample and the annotations as a whole class to check for understanding.
14. Pose these questions:

- Do we agree that this sentence follows the rules for writing that we know? How do you know? What makes you say that?
- Which words in this sentence make it interesting? Why are they interesting?
- What makes this writing easy to read? Anything else?

Teacher sample: success criteria courtesy of Aviva D.

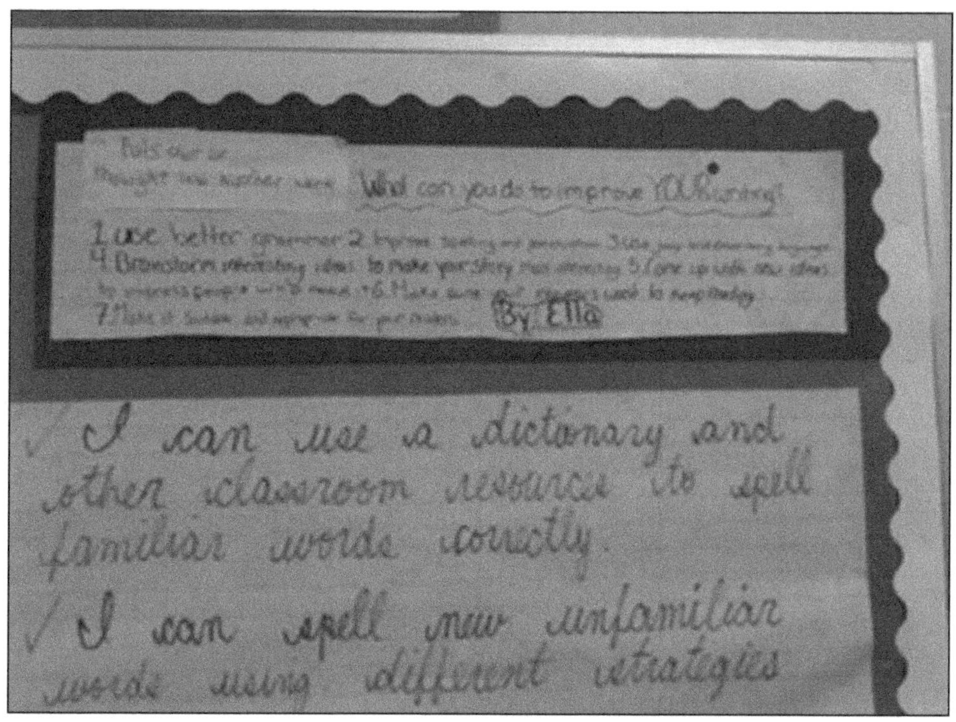

Pause and Ponder

Rick Stiggins (2012) suggests that we "eliminate the mystery surrounding the meaning of success in [our] classrooms by letting [our] students see [our] vision. If they can see it, they can hit it." (p. 68)

- How does this process of co-constructing success criteria remove the "mystery"?
- What are some questions you might have about leading this process?
- What resources (colleagues, books, videos) might support you?

Tips for Clarifying, Documenting, and Navigating the Learning Journey

- Share and clarify goals with students
- Keep goals visible and refer to them regularly
- Co-construct success criteria through use of samples
- Support goals by keeping success criteria visible
- Use samples of different levels of quality
- Ask students to match their work with samples
- Model for students how to use proof cards and connect to criteria for their own and peers' work
- Use physical and digital spaces to document and reflect on learning—*learning* or *living* walls; this is not a display, it is a support for learning
- Support students in becoming interested and invested in helping peers
- Provide adequate time for peer and self-assessment
- Use bump-it-up walls for peer and self-assessment and reflection
- Help students become their own best assessors and documenters of their learning, through the use of learning journals, portfolios, conferences

When we partner with our students in assessment, we help them gather and showcase evidence of their growth, through documenting their learning and reflecting on the learning strategies they are developing along the way. We help make the invisible processes of learning visible for our students. All these processes help us be responsive and differentiate in a meaningful, integrated way. They also support students' metacognitive growth and develop their self-efficacy. This is our ultimate learning goal—self-motivated, independent learners. These are life-long and transferable skills, and our students grow confidence and motivation through the very act of documenting and reflecting.

Meaningful classroom assessment centres students, from the beginning, in the assessment process and provides a variety of ways for students to show the full range of their learning.

Jay McTighe suggests that "greater attention must be given to gathering evidence of authentic student work through performance tasks and projects. By collecting authentic student work samples in digital portfolios, students can compile a literal 'album' of growth and evidence of genuine achievements over their school career." Further, he says that we need different kinds of evidence to "gauge different types of learning, we need a broader collection of measures, with a greater emphasis on authentic, performance-based projects." (McTighe, 2018)

Gathering Evidence and Triangulation

What kinds of evidence do you collect? Take a few moments to jot down all the different kinds of evidence of learning you are already gathering from students on a daily basis. You might wish to organize it using a triangle:

The Triangulation of Evidence.

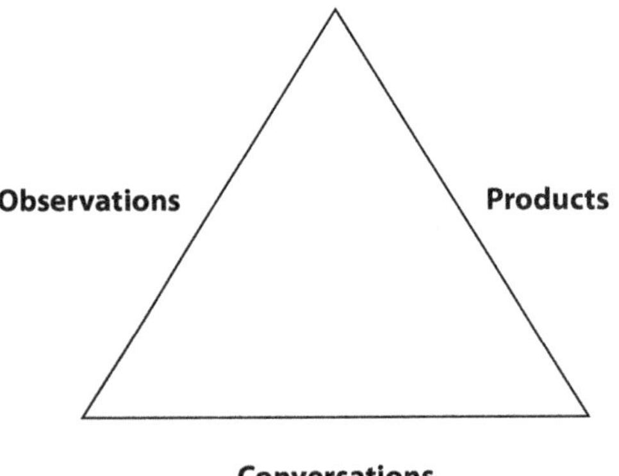

You will probably notice that you are collecting evidence from all these sources and that the evidence is informing your instructional decisions moment by moment, day by day. On the other hand, you might notice that you could curate a more complete picture of student understanding by having more opportunities to listen in and track student conversation or by allocating more time for focused observation. All these methods of gathering evidence can be integrated into the day, and you can provide just-in-time feedback to move learning forward in the moment, when it is most helpful in catching misunderstandings and providing scaffolding for the next stage of learning.

Pause and Ponder

A few questions to consider:

- Does the evidence you are connecting accurately reflect what you intended?
- Does it show the full range of student learning? Are there any limitations or restrictions that might be preventing students from showing what they know and can do?
- Is the evidence too much? Is it possible to see patterns in the evidence to help you in your planning?

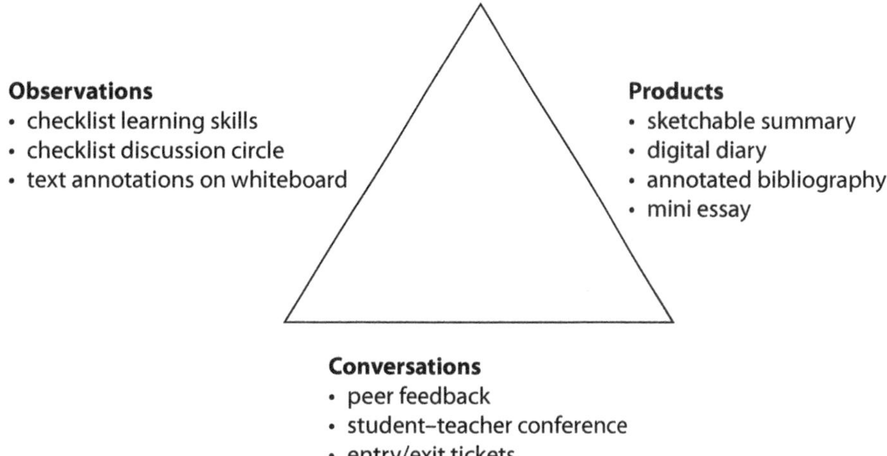

This approach to evidence collection supports our desire to form valid and reliable assessments of student learning progress. Note that the evidence is collected over time, in a variety of ways—Conversations, Observations, and Products—in which students are actively involved. This approach to gathering evidence helps us see and hear learning as it unfolds. We can start to see trends and patterns in the class and from each student. This approach to gathering evidence of student learning is called *triangulation*.

Take a moment here to refer back to your earlier reflection. You may have noticed that you have more products than conversations or observations. Keep in mind that this is not necessarily a problem; the balance will shift depending on the types of learning goals you are collecting evidence about. For example, quizzes provide strong evidence about the attainment-of-knowledge learning goals, whereas observations will yield important information about the attainment of skills. What is key is the evidence you are looking for at the time and ensuring that the task will reveal information about the intended learning goal. Ensuring that you have sufficient evidence of the right kind, related to the learning goals and collected over time, is at the heart of formative assessment. This approach allows you to differentiate and ensure that every student has an opportunity to demonstrate what they know and can do in a variety of modes.

As a teacher, I'm always looking for ways to engage students as active participants in their own learning. The following whiteboard responses from teacher candidates reflect the barriers that can get in the way of learning, both for themselves and their students. Knowing that these are common challenges for all learners, how might we plan intentionally to remove or diminish their impact?

What gets in the way of your learning or engagement in class?

repetitive – I already know it

I'm anxious about something outside of school – I can't focus

- my lack of confidence / fear of failure

- teacher doesn't know we are lost -

- going too quickly for us to understand

if the teacher doesn't seem interested – she is just going through the motions

- the topic or vocabulary is new and I don't have any background knowledge or experience with it

- the lesson or teacher is hard to follow – poorly organized - rambling

- if I feel that it's not okay to ask questions

Adapted from *The 4 C's: A routine for structuring a text-based discussion*, Project Zero, Harvard Graduate School of Education

Learning Journal: 4 C's Exit Ticket	
4 C's Thinking Routine	
Connections What connections do you draw between the content of this chapter and your own experience as an assessor and as a learner?	Challenge What ideas, positions, or assumptions do you want to challenge in this chapter?
Concepts What key concepts or ideas do you think are important and worth holding on to from this chapter?	Changes What changes in attitudes, thinking, or action are suggested by this chapter, either for you or others?

PART B

To Sit Beside: The Meaning and Practice of Assessment

> "Assessment for learning and assessment as learning are powerful practices in classroom assessment. They consist of the following five routines:
> 1. Clarifying, sharing, and understanding learning intentions (goals)
> 2. Engineering effective discussions, tasks, and activities that elicit evidence of learning (conversations, observations, products)
> 3. Providing feedback that moves learners forward
> 4. Activating students as learning resources for one another (collaboration and peer assessment)
> 5. Activating students as owners of their own learning (self assessment)"
>
> — Wiliam & Leahy (2015)

Clarity about the language of assessment is essential for educators, students, and families. Families have a right to know what their children are learning and how their progress is being measured. In Ontario, the foundational document in assessment, *Growing Success*, offers the following direction:

> Assessment for the purpose of improving student learning is seen as both "assessment *for* learning" and "assessment *as* learning". As part of *assessment for learning*, teachers provide students with descriptive feedback and coaching for improvement. Teachers engage in *assessment as learning* by helping all students develop their capacity to be independent, autonomous learners who are able to set individual goals, monitor their own progress, determine next steps, and reflect on their thinking and learning." — Ontario (2010, p. 28)

Assessment For Learning

This is ongoing assessment; it takes place before and during the learning. The primary user of this information is the teacher. These are the assessments we make moment by moment and day by day. These assessments help us understand what students already know and can do, and they guide our teaching decisions. These assessments are not graded, but are essential to student learning and teacher planning. When we assess learning, we uncover misconceptions, notice gaps in understanding, provide specific and descriptive feedback, and decide how best to move forward in our planning. This might require that we revisit a lesson for the whole class. Or we might discover that only a few students need a review of the learning; this can be done in a small-group context while the remainder of the class works independently or collaboratively to advance their learning.

Assessment for learning is also called diagnostic or formative assessment.

- **Diagnostic assessment** is gathered before instruction, so teachers can uncover instructional starting points. Teachers use this information to plan initial instruction and assessment tasks that allow them to monitor student progress. The frameworks of Universal Design for Learning and Differentiated Instruction help teachers design instruction that is inclusive and equitable.
- **Formative assessment** is gathered during the learning, and this information is used by teachers to see where students are in relation to the learning goals, and to provide descriptive feedback and next steps as they are used to improve performance. Teachers use this information to differentiate instruction and assessment during the learning.

Assessment As Learning

This is ongoing assessment. The primary user of this information is the student. It occurs when students are active participants in the learning process. Students have a clear understanding of the learning goals, consciously monitor their progress toward meeting those goals through the use of samples and success criteria, and provide feedback to themselves and others to improve their performance. Students then act on their own feedback, as well as feedback from their peers and teacher, to adjust their performance. This is a powerful process that enables students to become skillful, metacognitive learners. It leads to confidence, independence, and self-efficacy.

Assessment Of Learning

Also called *summative assessment/summative evaluation*, this happens near the end of a unit of study to determine what students know and can do. This information is used to inform guardians, schools, and boards of education where students are in relation to curriculum expectations at a particular point in time. It is used to make placement decisions in the next grade or institution, and for grading and reporting. In the past, much of our attention as teachers has been taken by evaluation: testing, grading, calculating, and reporting grades. We now know how important it is to involve our students in assessment before and during the learning, as well. Lorna Earl suggests a reconfigured model of assessment wherein the bulk of our assessment time is spent gathering and using assessment information to guide our instruction and to support student learning rather than just grading final products.

Adapted from *Assessment As Learning: Using Classroom Assessment to Maximize Student Learning* by Lorna Earl (2013)

Traditional Assessment Plan

ASSESSMENT OF LEARNING SUMMATIVE ASSESSMENT (80%)	Assessment **For** and **As** Learning (20%)

Reconfigured Assessment Plan

ASSESSMENT FOR AND AS LEARNING DIAGNOSTIC AND FORMATIVE ASSESSMENT (80%)	Assessment of Learning Summative Assessment (20%)

CHAPTER 5

Assessment For Learning: Diagnostic and Formative Strategies

Prompt for Reflection

"Formative assessments are not just for the students… the teachers also must have continual feedback to guide their instruction. These assessments do not have to be elaborate. For example a simple exit slip done every day, will reveal the likely misunderstandings and misconceptions that may block student progress. A forward-thinking teacher will check for the likely misunderstandings to be able to eliminate them."

— Grant Wiggins in Jonson (2013)

- Generate a list of all the ways students provide you with information that you use to guide your instruction. What have you found to be most useful in guiding your decision-making? What kind of information do you need more often?

Essential Questions

- How do we know where to start with our instruction?
- How do we use the feedback we receive from students—in the form of their questions, actions, and work products—to inform our instructional decisions at the moment?
- How can we use our assessments to truly enhance learning rather than just measure it?

There is no doubt that we have an abundance of information coming to us from our students continuously. They communicate their enthusiasm, their interest, and their lack thereof through their words, actions, and interactions in the classroom. All of this can be useful in helping us direct and redirect their attention. Conversations, observations, and products can be used in a timely way to enhance learning, especially when we are all clear about the learning goals and the success criteria. Making learning visible and audible is essential for us to know what students are thinking, and how they are processing and interacting with content to make meaning. It is also essential for students to develop the metacognitive habits of mind to assess their progress and make appropriate adjustments. Making time for thinking about our thinking in the midst of learning is a powerful driver for enhanced learning. It reinforces the importance of learning and moves students away from focusing on completion and just mindlessly going through the motions.

When we engage students in formative assessment strategies, we elicit the information we need to make decisions in a timely way. These strategies help us discover who is following the lesson and who has lost their way. They provide us with information about how well students have internalized the success criteria and help us make decisions about what feedback would be most helpful in this moment. We also learn if it is time to bring together a few students to reteach a concept or to provide enhancement for others. Everything students say, do, and produce is feedback for us as teachers.

Assessment for learning involves gathering evidence of learning, interpreting it, and acting on it. Both diagnostic and formative assessment fit into this category. Both help us make decisions that support student learning: diagnostic comes before we engage in a new learning cycle or unit of study, while formative comes in the midst of the learning. It is important to keep in mind that the assessment task itself (a quiz, a checklist, an essay, a speech) is not diagnostic, formative, or summative; it is our purpose in using it that determines its function. For example, if you have students do a quiz in math that was initially intended as a summative, you might uncover that a number of students were not ready. You can make the choice that the quiz will be used as formative and it will not be included in a grade. You are using information to guide your instruction as you provide an opportunity for reteaching and re-assessment to advance learning. This is why we check for understanding along the way and adjust accordingly.

Diagnostic Assessment

See *Learning for All* (Ontario, 2022).

There are many educational assessments that can be used to identify instructional starting points and to help us adjust or modify learning goals, as appropriate for the individual needs of our students. Some are very formal and tightly structured, whereas others are quite informal and take the form of conversations and interviews with families. There could also be professional assessments, such as speech and language, medical, and psychological assessments, providing information and/or diagnosis of specific conditions that affect learning. Information can be gathered about student knowledge in a specific subject area or more generally. And we can gather information from a variety of sources, including from the student, from the student's previous teachers, and from the student's parents, as well as from formal sources, such as school records and past report cards.

There are a few cautions here with regard to using information from a student's past academic history. Although it can be of great value, it can also be used to pigeonhole or lower expectations about a student's ability. A previous assessment could reflect a particular bias—cultural or linguistic—that hampered a student's performance. A student and family might have been in transit or in some challenging circumstances—poor health, job loss, etc.—that disrupted a student's education. The student might have been particularly anxious or stressed during an assessment, and therefore could not show what they actually knew and could do. This is not to discount the value of diagnostic assessment and information from a variety of sources; however, the most useful assessment is the one that reveals information we can glean and use in our classrooms to enable and enhance performance on a daily basis.

Questions to Guide Assessment Selection and Design

1. Is this a valid and useful tool
   - to uncover student understanding related to the learning goals?
   - to support my planning and instruction?
   - for these students/this student at this time?
2. How can I design this assessment to
   - reveal information about student strengths and funds of knowledge?
   - encourage student sense of belonging and confidence?
   - uncover misconceptions?
   - identify gaps in knowledge?
   - inform my instruction in the short term?
   - inform my long-term planning?
   - support assessment and learning conversations?
   - make thinking visible/audible?

Embedded Formative Assessment

Formative assessment has many forms, and there are many strategies that can be used for this purpose. We employ formative assessment to gauge where students are in the learning cycle/the unit, and also to understand our own impact. Embedded formative assessment is what helps us know if our students are making progress, and it helps us know if our instructional decisions are having the results that we hoped to achieve. You might remember having been in a classroom where the instructor carried on with the lesson without checking to see or hear if students were following the content. I have taught lessons and been surprised at the end to discover that students have taken away something I did not intend to teach, or that they have latched onto a very small idea that was peripheral to the intended learning. This is important information for me, as a teacher, and it is best for me to know about misunderstandings or gaps in the midst of the learning. These discoveries about student learning help me make decisions about where to go next in my instruction.

Dylan Wiliam's strategy of "engineering effective discussions, tasks and activities that elicit evidence of learning" (Wiliam and Leahy, 2015) encourages us to employ strategies that empower students as active agents in their learning.

Pause and Ponder

Take a moment here to revisit the list of observations, conversations, and products you created earlier on. You might note that you are already gathering lots of information about student learning that is very useful. The key here is to respond to the information in the midst of the learning by providing relevant, specific, and timely feedback.

Whole-Class Discussions and Effective Questioning

Teacher-led whole-class discussions can bring students into the learning and have them show what they know and understand in the moment. Although these might look effortless in the hands of a highly skilled teacher, they require planning to elicit the information we are seeking and also require planning from a psychological safety point of view. You likely recall feeling that it was safe to volunteer an answer to a teacher's question as a student in some classes, and you probably also recall the trepidation you felt elsewhere if a teacher called on you to answer. What led to that sense of trepidation? Maybe it was the subject matter, maybe it was the classroom dynamics, perhaps it was because you had been tuned out and didn't catch the first part of the lesson. There are many reasons why students do not participate in class discussions. On the other hand, we could have students in our class who wish to dominate the conversation and ask and answer all the questions. If we allow this to be the pattern for discourse, other students might choose to buy out completely.

"Quality questioning activates and sustains interactions and relationships between students and teachers, between students and content in ways that increase both student engagement and achievement."
— Walsh & Sattes, cited in *Adolescent Literacy Guide* (Ontario Ministry of Education, 2012)

How do we invite everyone into the conversation, make it safe to make mistakes, and continue to move the learning forward? As discussed in chapter 1, we create the climate for learning conversations by co-constructing classroom norms and coming back to them every day. Having them posted in our classrooms as environment nudges (see page 14) provides scaffolds and reminders for all. We can reinforce and support these norms through the use of stem starters on student desks or on a learning wall. These provide students with an entry into whole-class and small-group conversations.

Questions drive learning, and the more readily students can pose questions and pursue answers, the more they are likely to be motivated. Students need practice in framing questions and designing their own inquiries. There are many questioning frameworks available that can help us design questions that elicit specific cognitive skills or processes. Bloom's taxonomy is one helpful tool that prompts us to think about the range of cognitive processes involved in thinking; however, we need not approach questioning in a hierarchical structure, as learning does not move forward in a linear way. Starting with a question can help generate further questions, build curiosity, and heighten motivation.

Morgan and Saxton (2006) offer a helpful classification of questions organized around specific intentions. These can help us pose questions that uncover student knowledge and understanding, and also to build and shape thinking.

A Classification of Questions

Adapted from *Asking Better Questions* by Morgan and Saxton (2006)

Questions that Elicit Information	Questions that Shape Understanding	Questions that Press for Reflection
These questions expose what students already know and believe to be true. • They get at what is explicit.	These questions require students to make connections between content and their own understanding. They encourage students to express and elaborate on their ideas. • They start to get at what is implied or suggested but not stated explicitly.	These questions challenge students to engage critically and creatively with ideas and texts. • They move further into the ideas and ask us to take what we are learning and apply it in new ways.

Notes

- Each of these types of questions are equally important in the learning process.
- Research indicates that, in many classrooms, both student and teacher questions fall into the first category; i.e., eliciting information.
- Notice how the posing and extending of these questions is both an instructional and assessment strategy. Helping students generate a range of questions using this structure supports their development as meaning-makers and problem-posers. It positions them as active participants in their learning.

Pause and Ponder

It is estimated that teachers take up 10–20% of class time with questions (Carlsen, 1991) and ask about 120 questions in an hour (Vogler, 2008).

- Does this capture your experience as a student? teacher?

Have a look at the classification of questions on page 61:

- What kinds of questions support and build student thinking?
- What kinds of questions dominated your experience as a student? As a teacher?
- Which kinds of questions would you predict are most likely to be engaging for students?
- Which types of questions are likely to provide you with meaningful and relevant assessment information?

Strategy: Speech Balloons

Speech balloons support reflection and deepen cognitive engagement, as they provide a visible scaffold support to conversation and thinking, make individual thinking visible and accessible to all students, enable students to track their thinking, and revisit what helped them learn and show progression in posing questions and knowledge building (Frey, Hattie, & Fisher, 2018, p.149). The idea is to support students in internalizing the patterns of thinking and questioning that

- move learning forward
- reveal misconceptions and gaps in learning
- value contributions from all
- consider a variety of perspectives
- values curiosity over criticism

1. Place speech balloons around the room or on students' desks to help them enter into conversation and build on the thinking of their peers. See template on page 70.
2. Speech balloons can be tailored to suit the specific context and grade level. Some of the following might be a helpful start to support and clarify thinking moves:

   Adding and Building
   - I would like to add…
   - I think this (idea, comment, quotation, consideration) is important too.
   - How can we build on this idea?
   - What other evidence supports this thinking?

You might notice that many of these questions are generative or facilitative, rather than procedural or review. These types of questions invite and extend learning and help students pose questions to drive their own learning.

Clarifying
- I have a question about…
- Can you clarify?
- I'm not clear about…
- I think I get this:…. I'm not sure what's next.

Paraphrasing and Summarizing
- So, you are saying…
- Let me see if I've got this right:…

Challenging
- What about…?
- Is there another way we could look at this?
- What else might be true?
- Why do you think that?
- I'm wondering about…
- I have a question about…
- The muddiest point is…

Speech balloons can be supported with photographs of students in moments of dialogue. Although they may start up on the learning wall or on display, based on the teacher's modeling and words, eventually they can come to contain words actually spoken by students. We can add to the ones that we have created and ensure that students' authentic voices are recognized. We can ask students to create them by having them document

a) a question someone asked today that helped them think differently about an idea, or
b) a question they posed today that helped a peer move forward in their learning

Accountable Talk

Lucy West, internationally renowned educator and author, indicates that, in order to cultivate a culture of deep thinking and understanding in the classroom, it is essential to give "the weight in conversation to students not just the teacher." We know that listening to classroom talk enables us to understand student thinking and to make instructional decisions in the form of questions or scaffolded prompts that will help students progress.

Students also benefit from listening to their own ideas, as it helps them clarify their own thinking, and also question, build on, and extend the thinking of others. While teachers understand the many reasons dialogue and discourse are central to student engagement and understanding, barriers often prevent the practice of sustained, accountable talk and cooperative learning in the classroom. Time constraints, lack of emotional safety, and mistrust of others can often get in the way of our intention to invite and encourage deep thinking and discourse.

West advocates for the use of accountable talk in our classrooms to engage students, and nurture active and empowered participants able to formulate their own questions and direct their own inquiry. Cultivating this climate for accountable talk requires an environment of safety, a place where mistakes are welcomed and seen as a starting place for learning. As students continue to learn how to engage in these conversations, with teacher modeling and support, they learn how to make meaning of their learning and to think together to clarify understanding. These discussions provide teachers with the information they need to provide and differentiate feedback in the moment.

Strategy: Three Basic Talk Moves

This strategy provides three supportive talk moves that can be incorporated into whole-class discussion and also embedded in collaborative learning.

Adapted from Project Zero's Thinking Routine Toolbox (Harvard Graduate School of Education, 2022)

Turn and Talk

1. Turn to assigned elbow partner.
2. Take turns sharing your ideas.
3. Help each other: add, build, suggest.

Repeat That

Ask your partner or a member of the whole-class discussion to repeat a response to a question:

Could you please repeat that?

Say More about That

Encourage your partner or someone else in the whole-class discussion to share more about their idea.

Pause and Ponder

Take a moment here to reflect on the following quotations on the importance of student talk and the essential practices of observing and listening for learning. Follow up by completing Claim, Support, Add, Question.

> "Accountable talk refers to the ways that teachers skillfully encourage their students to think deeply, articulate their reasoning and listen with a purpose. It is shaped by the tasks in which students engage as well as by the nature of the learning environment."
> — Lucy West

> "Circulating as students work in pairs or groups, teachers often arrive in the middle of an activity. Too often they immediately ask children to explain what they are doing. Doing so may not only be destructive but may also cause teachers to miss wonderful moments for assessment. Listening carefully first is usually more helpful, both to find out how students are thinking and to observe how they are interacting."
> — Storeygard, Hamm, & Fosnot (2010)

> "Never say anything a kid can say! This one goal keeps me focused. Although I do not think that I have ever met this goal completely in any one day or even in a given class period, It has forced me to develop and improve my questioning skills. It also sends a message to students that their participation is essential. Every time I am tempted to tell students something, I try to ask a question instead."
> — Reinhart (2000, p. 480)

> **Teacher Strategy: Claim, Support, Add, Question**
>
> 1. Claim: After reading the three quotations, summarize the claims the authors are making.
> 2. Support: Summarize the evidence the authors present to support their claims.
> 3. Add: Build on these ideas by adding from your own classroom experience of questioning and accountable talk.
> 4. Question: Generate a question related to the claims. What is still unclear? What more do you need to know?

Strategy: Claim, Support, Add, Question

This thinking routine can be used in the classroom to have students think deeply about texts they are reading, viewing, or listening to. Depending on the grade level, model and provide guided practice of the process. Explain what it means to *make a claim, provide evidence,* and *build knowledge.* Supporting this learning with examples at various levels will help students understand the criteria and work towards it. Notice how effectively this thinking routine makes the pattern of accountable talk, thinking, and writing visible.

1. Claim: Summarize the claims the author is making.
2. Support: Summarize the evidence the authors present to support their claims.
3. Add: Build on these ideas by adding from your own experience of questioning and accountable talk.
4. Question: Generate a question related to the claims. What is still unclear? What more do you need to know?

Embedded Formative Assessment Tips

Foundations and Gathering Evidence

- Mistakes are expected and lead to learning.
- Help students understand that mistakes lead to learning and that teachers need to know where they are so they can support them in moving forward.

Co-construct Norms

- Establish norms for class discussion: all responses are welcomed; students listen and learn together; feedback is immediate and responsive to students' answers. Teachers acknowledge what is correct and provide additional questions to build on and probe responses. Students also contribute to the learning by clarifying and adding their own questions.

Pacing of Questions and Responding to Answers

When teachers extend wait time, students' responses improve in quality and detail, and more students are willing to participate. Wait time can be extended even more if you build in time for a Think–Pair–Share or a quick write.

> Wait Time 1: Teacher provides sufficient wait time for students to process the question before taking any responses. A 3–5 second pause is sufficient.

Wait Time 2: the time after a student's response that allows processing and encourages other students an opportunity to think about their classmate's answer

Both kinds of wait time create a thinking culture and build a community of learners and listeners.

Strategies for Increasing Accountability and Participation

No Hands Up and Popsicle Sticks

Reminders: Pose question first, then select the student's name. The student's name goes back into the cup after being called as we want to keep them involved in the learning.

This strategy addresses the issue of the same students answering all the questions and some students disengaging entirely. It ensures that everyone is listening to the question as they may be called upon to answer. It also helps the teacher track how the instruction is landing with students.

1. Students are not to raise their hands to answer a question. Teacher will select students at random. This can be done just by putting students' names on popsicle sticks and pulling them out randomly.
2. Students might feel some anxiety, but once the teacher's intention is clear—to assess what students know and to inform their teaching—anxiety will lessen. Students have a right to pass if they are not ready to answer.
3. Teacher takes a few more answers and then returns to students who may have passed. They can then repeat something they have heard, add to what has been shared, or ask for clarification.

Call Upon A Friend

This strategy can be added as a way to help students who feel stumped. They can call upon a friend who has not yet participated in the discussion to speak on their behalf. You can come back to the person who passed it on to check for understanding.

Strategies for Checking In and Checking for Understanding

All these strategies help us listen in, document learning, build understanding, and engage students cognitively and socially. After using these strategies, it is often very useful to debrief the processes used in cooperative learning by asking students to answer the following:

- What learning skills and habits of mind helped you collaborate effectively?
- What learning skills and habits of mind did your collaborators use effectively?
- How did this task/process/strategy help you move toward the learning goals and/or part of the success criteria?

Students can make a note in their learning journal and perhaps support it with an artifact from their work. This helps them build the metacognitive habit and see that they are making progress.

Fist To Five

This can be used as a quick check in with students. A closed fist means "I'm not sure what we are doing"; an open hand with all five fingers out indicates the student is with you and understands completely; fingers can be held up to indicate how much the student understands.

This doesn't provide specific information about what is understood; however, it can provide helpful information about the class as a whole. Encourage students to hold their hand in front of their chest to give you an indication. Of course, some students might just say what others in the class are saying, so this is not the most reliable indicator.

This strategy can also be used to take a read of the room in terms of social-emotional readiness for learning. If the entire class is indicating 3 or below, there may need to be a quick body break energizer, a mindful moment, or a class conversation. This is important assessment information that we can use to regroup and reestablish a positive climate for learning.

Mini-Whiteboards

Students can share their thinking through the use of small whiteboards and teachers can get a quick update about what students understand and can do.

Random Grouping, Sharing a Marker, and Non-Permanent Vertical Whiteboards

Developed by Peter Liljedahl in *Building Thinking Classrooms in Mathematics* (2001).

In this strategy, students are randomly assigned to work in groups of two or three: Peter Liljedahl's research (2021) suggests that K–2 work in pairs and Grade 3 and up worked best in groups of three. Groups can be involved in solving a problem, annotating a text, or responding to a prompt.

1. In random groups, students address a variety of questions on vertical whiteboards.
2. They share out to the whole class.
3. As a result of the sharing, they add to their answers/proposed courses of action.

Try this in any subject area.

A key part of the strategy is that students are standing at a non-permanent vertical whiteboard: research suggests that students are more willing to expose their thinking on the whiteboard, as they are working through their ideas, if they know they can correct their work in the moment. It is erasable so, as the group thinking evolves, it can be adjusted. In addition, students practice taking turns sharing the marker and building their answer together.

Although this strategy was designed for the math classroom, it can be adapted in many content areas. The whiteboards allow for movement and group problem-solving in the classroom. In addition to the benefits in thinking, increased willingness to collaborate, elimination of social barriers, increased knowledge mobility, increased enthusiasm for learning, and reduced social stress were also seen (Liljedahl, 2021).

Teacher candidates generating proposed approaches to problems of practice that they encountered during their placements.

Sketchnote and/or $1 Summary

Students have a very short period of time to summarize what they have learned so far. This can be done as a sketchnote and/or a $1 summary (10 words only).

Turn and Talk

This is exactly as it suggests: two or three students share their thinking and come back to the big group. This is nicely paired with the creation of a Tweet, which can be posted to capture and document the learning.

Dotmocracy

Teacher distributes the same number of different-colored dots and students use them to vote on a group of alternatives or options. It could be used to select among options of solutions to various kinds of problems or courses of actions. It could be used to self-assess understanding of success criteria.

Red might indicate disagreement or lack of understanding.
Green might indicate agreement or complete understanding.

This is a versatile and manageable strategy to encourage students to think through options, share their opinions visibly, and get a sense of the group's response or level of understanding.

Index Card Summaries/Questions

Students can summarize or pose questions on index cards. These are excellent as tickets out the door and can help you prepare for feedback the next day.

Parking Lot

Create a space in the classroom for students to post questions during the lesson. You can access these while students are working in groups or independently, and address them in whole-class conversation or individually as required.

Inside/Outside Circle

This is an effective practice to build knowledge and to uncover what students are thinking during class. Once again, students can be called at random, as they have had the opportunity for conversation and can share an idea they learned during the conversation. You can also observe how students are interacting with one another, and perhaps notice those who need additional support. This strategy also builds the relationships and confidence necessary to engage students in more complex collaborative learning and assessment.

This can be noisy and requires space to organize students. You might need to reorganize furniture to make space. An alternative is to have students line up facing each other in two rows of seats. After the initial round, one row moves down 3 seats and everyone has a new partner.

1. Assign each student a number *1* or *2*. All the *1*s form a circle facing out; all the *2*s form an outside circle facing a partner in the inside circle.
2. Students take turns sharing their responses to a prompt from the teacher.
3. After one minute, the inner circle moves three spaces to the left. New partnerships are formed and the teacher provides a new prompt for discussion related to the lesson.
4. When students return to their seats, the teacher debriefs the conversations and summarizes the content on the board.

Learning Journal: Graphic Organizer to Summarize Thinking

- Use the triangle to identify something that was pointed out to you in this chapter. It could be something new, a reminder, a practice that you learned more about. It is something you want to remember.
- Use the circle to identify something that is still going around in your head. This could be something surprising, confusing, impactful, important.
- Use the square to identify something that squares with your thinking. This is something you agree with. It makes sense to you; it has value and meaning for you.

Speech Balloons

CHAPTER 6

Assessment For Learning: Feedback for Growth

Prompt for Reflection

"All students (as all teachers) do not always succeed the first time, nor do they always know what to do next, nor do they always attain perfection. This is not a deficit or, deficit thinking, or concentrating on the negative; rather, it is the opposite in that acknowledging errors allow for opportunities."
— Hattie (2012)

"A classroom is a place where a community of learners—as opposed to a collection of discrete individuals—engages in discovery and invention, reflection and problem-solving."
— Kohn (1999, p. 3)

- What connections do you make between these two quotations? How do they amplify the need for a positive climate for learning?

Essential Questions

- How do we provide effective, descriptive feedback during the learning?
- How can we maximize opportunities for direct observation and assessment conversations during the learning?

Feedback that comes after a performance is generally not valued by students. If it comes to them too late to improve the outcome they often prize most, i.e., the grade, then it is rarely used. Unfortunately, this is quite common in our schools, whether elementary, secondary, or post-secondary. Many students are focused on grading rather than learning. This is the case largely because teachers are required to calculate and submit grades for reporting purposes. This is not the entire issue, though. Part of the issue is the need for coverage of content and a desire to verify that learning has taken place. Formative assessment, specifically the effective use of just-in-time feedback, can help us address both of these challenges. We can help students see the connection between their efforts and their learning when we provide feedback they can use to actually improve their performance.

The graphic below shows the recursive nature of learning and growing. Each spiral builds on the one before so that what we feed back is fed-forward into new learning. Notice how each element aligns with the key strategies of Backward Design from Chapter 3.

Clarifying goals and purposes: *Where are we going and why are we going?*

Planning: *What evidence will show us that we are making progress?*

Execute, Assess, and Gather Evidence: *How will we gather the evidence?*

Examine, Reflect, and Generate Feedback: *Where are we now?*

Act on Feedback to Modify Performance: *What are our next steps based on the evidence?*

Revisit/Clarify Goals and Purposes: *Where to next?*

Assessment For/As Learning Feedback Spirals

Inspired by Costa & Kallick (2009)

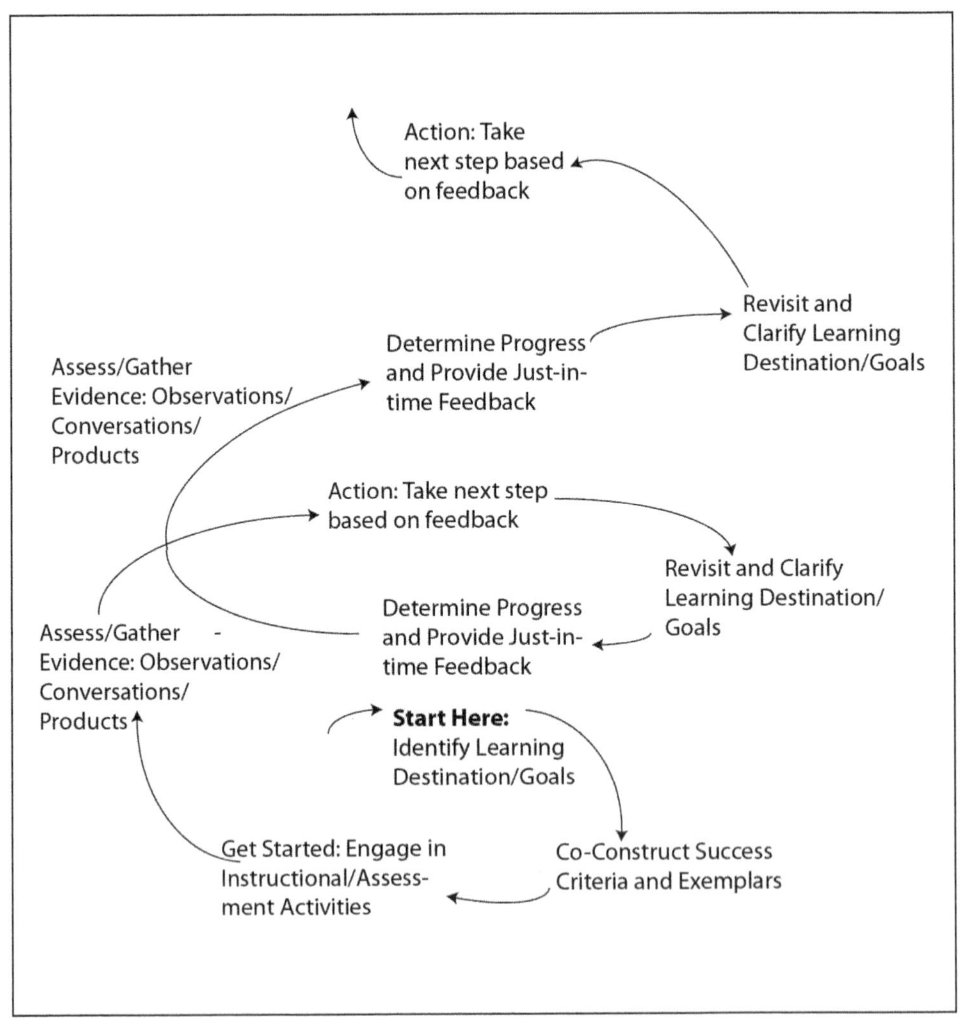

Pause and Ponder

What are the qualities of feedback that really make a difference? What feedback have you received that helped you grow and gave you a sense of optimism and confidence as a learner?

During the COVID-19 pandemic, I took a year-long training through the Centre for Compassion and Altruism. This program involved the development of a Capstone Project to bring the science of compassion into various fields of community involvement and the workplace. This is a global program that brings together people from diverse backgrounds, communities, and professions, who share a common desire to learn and to contribute positively in the world: a key goal is to take action to alleviate suffering. We worked collaboratively and independently to design, develop, refine, and enact our projects. We met regularly in large and small groups to learn together and to share our learning together. A key feature was sharing our projects and then receiving "appreciative feedback." These meetings involved sharing our progress in small groups and hearing specific and detailed feedback on the strengths of our work from every member of the small group. Every participant was invited to be attentive to the unfolding of the short presentation by the creator of the project. After receiving this encouragement as presenters, we had an opportunity to ask for advice or to invite questions or suggestions for next steps. This was the most effective learning experience I have ever had. I sensed others were interested in the outcome and I valued their expertise. I was interested in their feedback and I used it to refine and enhance my work. I learned from their experiences and their learning added to mine.

I share this story because I think it illustrates what we want for our students. We want them to develop a sense of ownership, efficacy, identity, and empowerment through their learning. Our aim is to develop their confidence and competence to make a positive contribution to society. We know that effective feedback supports improved performance, but only if it is valued, heard, and acted upon. The context for feedback and the positive impact that feedback can have is contingent on many factors: relationship, timing, relevance, specificity, usefulness, and amount. What is powerful here is that the learner, the creator of the work, requests the feedback about a specific aspect that is worrisome or unclear. This brings about powerful results. The feedback changes the direction of the learning and adds to the quality of the outcome. How can we approximate this sort of learning in our classrooms on a regular basis? What conditions lead to this development of self-efficacy and engagement?

Rick Stiggins (2012) points to the importance of the link between student self-concept, academic self-efficacy, and student success. He says, "Those who see themselves as capable learners are predisposed to be capable learners." Perhaps you have noticed this in your own classroom. Confident students feel that they can improve and so they act on feedback; students lacking in confidence and with a history of academic challenges might feel it isn't worth putting in the effort to read or learn from the feedback. Sometimes giving up is communicated by truancy, disruptive behavior, or feigned lack of interest. It can certainly save face to pretend you don't care, rather then risk public failure. This attitude often leads to further disengagement, poor attendance, and isolation, and has a negative impact on literacy development and eventually life outcomes. Assessment for Learning practices can help students move forward and start to build a sense of efficacy.

Pause and Ponder

Bring to mind two students you are teaching now—one who is confident, intrinsically motivated, and progressing very well, and another who is unsure, hesitant, perhaps even disengaged. How have the academic histories of these two students contributed to their attitudes toward learning? How do these attitudes affect their current academic achievement and their emotional well-being? How can we have a positive impact on both and keep them advancing toward their learning goals?

Students who receive assessment information that confirms they are on the right track, moving forward, come to see themselves as active agents in their learning. When students get this feeling of empowerment and self-efficacy as a result of receiving continuous evidence of success from assessment information, they start to experience hope and optimism, ready to follow up on feedback with productive action. They are on an upward spiral. They often engage in positive self-talk, such as, "I've got this!" "I'm making progress!" "My efforts are paying off." They might embrace habits of mind like Persisting and Responding with Wonderment and Awe.

When students are in the upward spiral they start to develop an internal sense of locus of control, seeing that outcomes are within their power. They are more confident, more engaged, more resilient, and more likely to apply meaningful effort. And the motivation can actually be about the learning, not the grade!

Pause and Ponder

Have you noticed these attributes in your students and in yourself? Do you recall a particular moment in education when you felt this or witnessed this strong and affirming sense of accomplishment?

We all want to be on the rise, to see that our efforts matter and pay off in some way, such as reaching a goal, developing a talent, having a sense of matter and meaning, etc. When we have this experience, we are encouraged to keep moving and to see that our actions and beliefs influence our results. This internal locus of control, the belief that our achievements are tied to our actions, is essential to success.

"Expectations about the likelihood of eventual success determine the amount of effort people are willing to put in. Those who are convinced that they can be successful in carrying out the actions required for a successful outcome—who have the 'self-efficacy'—are likely to try harder and to persist longer when they face obstacles."
— Kanter (2024)

The alternative belief, that something outside of us—other people or circumstances—determine our outcomes, removes this sense of control and can leave us feeling diminished, hopeless. Of course, some things are not within our control, but many are. How we respond to challenges and feedback makes a difference. If we cultivate a growth mindset to see that we can learn and try new things, we are shifting the sense that things are beyond our influence. The feedback that we provide to students can help them see that they are on their way, that they might not be there yet, but they are making progress. This is the power of helping students stay on upward spirals and preventing downward trajectories of disengagement. Our assessment practices are about cultivating hope, building resilience, and recognizing the value of intentional practice and reflection.

Effective Formative Feedback

So, what constitutes effective formative feedback? What qualities make it most likely to have a positive impact on student learning? As Chappuis (2021, p. 56) says, "Effective feedback acts like a global positioning system for students telling them how close they are to the target and what steps they can take to reach it." Research from a variety of sources suggest the following characteristics of effective descriptive feedback:

- It connects to the learning goals and related success criteria.
- It points out the strengths of the work.
- It points out the effective use of processes or strategies—a habit of mind/disposition or a learning skill (persistence, perspective-taking, problem-solving, organization, collaborative skills, independence, etc.).
- It notes what is absent or incorrect.
- It provides one or more of the following:
  - a correction
  - a specific feature that needs work
  - direction about what to do next
  - a "closing the gap" prompt
  - a reminder prompt for a student who might have just overlooked an element; this student is likely very close to meeting the goal
  - a scaffolded prompt (more than a reminder) for a student on their way to the goal who requires more direction; could be in the form of a question, a direction, a stem starter
  - an example prompt, referring back to exemplars, connecting to criteria, annotating a problem, thinking aloud, demonstrating, etc.
    (adapted from Shirley Clarke 2001)

- It is provided in the "right dose": the right amount, at the right time, for the specific student and learning context (Hattie and Clarke, 2019).
- Its purpose is to provide direction; it is most effective when provided without any level or grade.
- It does not do the thinking for the student (Chappuis, 2021).

In sum, powerful feedback provides information about how well the learning goals have been achieved through the task and it provides information about the thinking processes and strategies that the student has used to approach the task. It helps the student focus on the learning itself and the effectiveness of the approach. Hattie and Timperley (2007) speak to these important levels of feedback: about the task, the processing, and the learner's self-regulation (persistence, monitoring, metacognition, self-assessment, self-appraisal, self-management, etc.), and explain that feedback framed in this way is powerful. They also point to another level of feedback—about the self—that is ineffective and can in fact hinder progress and student learning. Self feedback focuses on the learner themselves rather than the work. For example, "You are so clever!" "You're terrific!" "Superstar!" Feedback about the self does not have task-related information and cannot be used to advance learning. In fact, it can contribute to a fixed mindset, in which a student believes they are naturally smart and need not put in effort to reach goals. This can be very limiting to the student when they meet a challenge and can't get it right. We move away from contributing to this fixed sense of self toward a growth mindset when we point to the processes and strategies they have used well in approaching the task; this also helps students see the value of acting on the feedback. (Dweck, 2006)

"So what should we say when children complete a task—say, math problems—quickly and perfectly? Should we deny them the praise they have earned? Yes. When this happens, I say, 'Whoops. I guess that was too easy. I apologize for wasting your time. Let's do something you can really learn from!'"
— Dweck (2006)

The quote in the margin speaks to the importance of gathering assessment information and using it to design instruction that is differentiated based on the knowledge of instructional starting points for the student. When we construct effective formative feedback with these qualities in mind, we can see powerful shifts in student engagement, achievement, and sense of efficacy. They know what they have done well and they know what to do next to improve. Unfortunately, I think what is often overlooked in our assessment practice is the timing of sharing the information with students and the provision of class time for students to actually receive the feedback, have time to digest it, ask questions about it, and then apply it to improve performance in real time.

Pause and Ponder

How do you already make time, space, and opportunity to provide feedback in a timely and powerful way?

Early in my teaching career, it was my practice to return work to students near the end of the class period. This meant that it was often rushed and students tossed it into binders without time to look it over, especially if it was formative rather than summative. It took time for me to see that the practice of "coaching for performance" in my drama class could be transferred to my English and Marketing classes. We could make time for rehearsal, for practice, feedback, and reflection, if we were worked through our learning and application in class. The active practices of reading, listening, speaking, presenting, and meaning-making of the drama classroom could be applied elsewhere. This would lead to more active student involvement, collaboration, self-efficacy, and motivation.

Cooperative Learning, Collaborative Skills and Assessment Conversations

Cooperative learning provides us with many opportunities to listen in on student conversations and to look at what they are producing, both individually and collectively. Many researchers have pointed out the necessity for students to engage in meaning-making collaboratively; learning is social. Both Hattie and Marzano point to the value of engaging students directly with content, revisiting material over time, applying what is being learned, and constructing understanding together.

Cooperative learning adds value to individual and whole-class instruction. Cautions from these researchers and others remind us of the importance of structuring work effectively and teaching collaborative skills, in order for groups to function well. In cooperative learning approaches, we are working toward the achievement of academic and social, emotional, relational skills. We work toward helping students build relationships, have a sense of belonging, and make contributions to their own learning and the learning of the entire community. (See Chapters 1 and 2 for specific approaches to building a learning community.) Here we will explore how we continue to build this positive and encouraging climate for deep learning and active student participation. When students are actively engaged in their work, we can have a powerful impact as we listen in and coach from the sidelines.

Johnson's 5

There are many strategies we can select from to engage students in interesting and relevant group work. We can also combine many strategies to foster thinking and communication skills that are transferable to other contexts. Johnsons' 5 Basic Elements of Group Work are foundational to effective learning. These are shown in the diagram below.

Bennett and Roleheiser (2001) provide a summary of each of these essential elements.

As we are designing tasks for students to work on collaboratively, it is important to build in **Individual Accountability**. How will each student contribute to the learning? What roles can be assigned to students to help them see that they belong and they are making a valuable contribution?

The **Collaborative Skills**—listening, speaking respectfully, pausing, paraphrasing, sharing resources, disagreeing agreeably, conflict resolution, etc.—must be taught early on and revisited as students develop. In addition, many students will need additional support in self-management, attentional focus, social-emotional self-regulation, etc. All these skills are important and foundational to student achievement and well-being; they are also highly prized transferable skills.

Ideally, work is done in a physical or online environment that allows for meaningful interaction and dialogue. Recently, I have noticed that many students struggle to engage in conversation with their peers, both online and in person. Taking the time to build relationships and brave spaces for sharing ideas is key to effective collaboration. Students will need explicit instruction and reminders about the skills of collaboration and productive group work. They will participate in co-constructing and refining the success criteria as they are learning and developing their skills. This element of Johnson's 5 is called **Face to Face Interaction**. We can also make use of this element online when we have students work in break-out rooms, in pairs, triads, groups of four. This will require reminders, prompts, and coaching to help students fully invest in the learning of the community. Some students will find this more difficult online and others will manage well. We need to coach both. Developing the skills of collaboration and interdependence will also help students become effective peer and self-assessors. As indicated earlier, making thinking visible and audible by having students interact in random groupings of three using vertical whiteboards (see page 67) is an excellent strategy to build in this face-to-face work and to support teachers and students in seeing the learning unfold.

Positive Interdependence is built into effective task design when we ensure that the outcome of the learning is a shared responsibility and the learning comes back to the learning community. Students depend on one another to accept individual accountability and to contribute to the whole. Using numbered heads to assign specific roles in groups can be a very effective organizational tool. For example, number students 1, 2, and 3, with 1 as the recorder, 2 as the problem-poser, 3 as the researcher. Roles are dependent on the specifics of the task, but having a clear role supports accountability and interdependence.

Direct instruction and building in assessment and reflection about the habits of mind one exhibited during a collaborative process can be an excellent tool for self-reflection and group-processing reflection. We can ask students to connect to criteria by asking "What is the evidence that you demonstrated this particular habit of mind?" or "What habit of mind might have been helpful here?"

Finally, and most importantly, is taking the time to process how well the group worked together to complete the task, **Processing the Group's Social and Academic Effort**. This reflective process is challenging, and sometimes students shy away from it, either because they know they did not live up to their responsibilities or because they are fearful about holding their group members accountable to the learning. You can provide tools for reflection that help students negotiate this together. You might even ask students to write a summary of their contributions and share them with the group. This can promote meaningful and honest dialogue about commitment to the learning and to the team.

It is important to be clear that we are required to teach communication and collaborative skills in many of our content standards; in Ontario, for example, we teach listening, speaking, and presenting as part of the Language curriculum. We assess and ultimately evaluate these skills across many content areas as integral to communication of student learning. They are intended to be taught explicitly and they are also transferable skills. We also assess collaboration as a learning skill. We track observations of students in collaborative experiences and also provide feedback to help them improve. When the time comes to analyze all the evidence we have of student learning over time, we can triangulate our observations, conversations, and products to evaluate the current achievement of students as listeners, speakers, presenters, and collaborators. What we document from all these experiences helps us provide a valid and reliable grade that is based on the evidence; the repeated opportunities to learn, practice, get feedback, and refine performance contributes to the depth of understanding and the ability to apply the learning. Cooperative learning opportunities provide these practice experiences and provide us with opportunities to see rich demonstrations of learning. We can measure the achievement of a content standard and the demonstration of the ability to collaborate.

Habits of Mind

Costa and Kallick refer to habits of mind as "a link among the various disciplines" that help students "find connections, bridges and unifying themes of learning across content areas" (2009, p.7). These 16 habits provide a framework for developing dispositions that enable academic performance and develop important skills. They are

Applying Past Knowledge to New Situations
Creating/Imagining/Innovating
Finding Humor

Gathering Data through All Your Senses
Listening with Empathy and Understanding
Managing Impulsivity
Persisting
Questioning and Posing Problems
Remaining Open to Continuous Learning
Responding with Wonderment and Awe
Striving for Accuracy
Taking Responsible Risks
Thinking About Your Thinking
Thinking and Communicating with Clarity and Precision
Thinking Flexibly
Thinking Interdependently

We can help students draw upon these habits as they engage in their learning and start to know themselves as learners. When we share, discuss, and apply the habits in our classroom, we are helping make tangible what is often mysterious. These habits can become a tool for self-assessment and metacognition: *Which habits of mind do you think are strengths for you? Which habits do you think you might want to work on? Which habit might help you as you work on this task today?* They can also be used as a backdrop to learning in literature and social studies: *What habits of mind did this character draw upon to help him achieve his goals? What habit of mind could have been useful to bring about a more peaceful and kind resolution?*

See page 91 for a reproducible representation of the Habits of Mind.

Building these habits into cooperative learning experiences enables students to learn about them and apply them over time. They can be posted as anchor charts and referred to regularly to underpin the learning goals and success criteria of the curriculum. Just as we co-construct success criteria for learning goals, we can co-construct success criteria for habits of mind and refer back to them to assess and monitor our progress.

Considerations for Grouping

Research by Liljedahl (2021) indicates the power of random grouping in mathematics Kindergarten to Grade 12. It is fascinating to hear how students responded to being assigned to groups randomly. In interviews, students revealed that they did not believe they were randomly assigned to groups by teachers, so Lilijedahl and team made the random grouping visible by assigning students using a card deck. Making the random grouping transparent to students changed their perception and engagement.

> "Although randomizing wrested the control from the teachers, making it visibly random was necessary for the students to both perceive and believe the randomness." — Liljedahl (2021, p. 45)

In his work, Liljedahl also points to research on the importance of groups being generative, and the need for both redundancy and diversity (Davis & Simmt, 2003). *Redundancy* here "reflects things that a group of students has in common—language, interests, experiences, knowledge"; whereas *diversity* points to things that are not held in common, such as "different ideas, viewpoints, perspectives" (Liljedahl, 2021, p. 45). We need both elements for groups to work productively: some commonality to begin collaborating, and diversity to create, produce, and generate thinking. When students self-select groups, there is a tendency for the groups to lack diversity, which diminishes the group's opportunities for exchanging and grappling with ideas.

Based on Liljedahl (2021, p. 49)

Assigning students frequently and randomly in Mathematics classrooms resulted the following gains:

- an increase in the number of students offering ideas
- an increase in willingness to collaborate (openness to others)
- an increase in knowledge mobility (random groupings helps remove barriers to knowledge moving between groups)
- a decrease in social barriers (friend and affinity groups, social structures that can be barriers to collaboration, began to fall away)
- increased enthusiasm for learning
- reduced social stress

For more on the specifics of this work in mathematics, see *Building Thinking Classrooms in Mathematics Grades K–12.* It is an excellent resource with applications for pedagogy across the curriculum.

Creating the structures and building the processes for students to collaborate productively not only accelerates learning, it helps us see learning in action and position students as active participants in their own learning as supports for one another.

Cooperative Strategies

These strategies offer opportunities to learn the skills of collaboration through practicing the skills of collaboration. You will be able to adapt for your specific context, i.e., your students, grade level, subject, etc. Some strategies are more suited to Social Science, Art, or Language and Literacy, and some might work most effectively in cross-curricular contexts.

Strategy: Paraphrase and Summarize

This strategy provides opportunities for students to practice listening and speaking, using success criteria, and self- and peer assessment. This strategy is useful and flexible. It can be used to summarize course content or to activate prior knowledge. It can also be returned to regularly and refined to add additional criteria, such as building on an idea, rebuttal, perspective taking, role-playing, etc.

1. Teacher provides an interesting topic or question to take turns listening and talking about. This can be related to an issue that has come up in class, the news, or something that they are keen to discuss. You might also offer choices so the pairs pick their topic.
2. Students jot down a few points they want to talk about.
3. Students face one another and letter off A and B
4. A speaks first to make their point: 1 minute.
5. B retells what A has said and aims to make it a little shorter. The idea is to practice paraphrasing.
6. A gives B feedback on the accuracy of what they have paraphrased, using the success criteria.
7. B thanks A and then responds to the feedback, perhaps asking for a suggestion for improvement.
8. Reverse roles. B becomes the speaker and A the listener, still on the same topic. B might choose to stick to their prepared notes and perhaps try to integrate some of what A has shared.
9. A summarizes, paraphrasing if possible.
10. B provides feedback to A, using the success criteria.

Tips for Implementation

- Start with something the students want to talk about.
- Model it with a student for the class and have students identify the criteria.

What did the listener do?
What did the speaker do?

- Keep it short.
- Refine it as you go.
- Including descriptive feedback is key. After students have practiced a few times, debrief the conversations. What was challenging? What was effective? What did they notice about their attention? How will this help them learn?
- Depending on the group, it might be appropriate to just retell directly, rather than paraphrase. Many students will be able to paraphrase, some will be challenged to be precise and concise. These are all teaching points and important for us to notice as teachers.

Assessment Opportunities

Pick one or two pairs to focus on. Use the success criteria to note observations for the pairs. Ask students to share their own observations and document them in their learning journal with a sticky note or check mark. Although this is a quick self-report, it provides some evidence of where they think they are as listeners and speakers, and can be discussed at a later date.

Extension

Create groups of four from the pairs. Have them redo the exercise with a new topic. This time one pair does the whole exercise while the second pair watches to provide feedback. Then the second pair does it and the first pair observes and provides feedback.

Payoff

Students will practice and internalize effective speaking and listening. They will be actively engaged in supporting each other as learners. They will practice the use of success criteria and giving feedback.

Strategy: Four Corners

This strategy allows students opportunities to talk to one another about interesting ideas, hear other perspectives, make connections, and build knowledge and understanding. It can be used anywhere in the learning cycle, depending on the learning goals. It can be used early on to get a sense of students' opinions and prior knowledge. It can be used to check understanding and build connections between students during learning, and is also very useful as a summary of learning to draw conclusions.

1. Teacher selects a number of relevant quotations, themes, images that connect to learning goals.
2. Students are told the purpose of the strategy: to hear a variety of responses and to extend our thinking.

3. Teacher previews the content to be placed in each corner (perhaps on a slide show). Students are allowed a little time to look over the images or prompts.
4. Teacher reads aloud quotations, clarifies vocabulary, checks for clarity, asks if there are questions about the meaning of the quotations.
5. Content is placed in the corners of the room. Students select the one that is most relevant/interesting to them and then move to that corner for a conversation and to explain their thinking.
6. Once students move to a particular corner, they break into smaller groups of two or three to explain their connections and hear from others. Teacher checks to see that everyone has a small group and joins in if someone is on their own.
7. Time is provided for the conversation. Depending on the age and level of engagement of students, this might be 2–6 minutes.
8. The class is called back together and teacher asks for a few responses from each group. Students are asked to share what they heard rather than what they said. This encourages students to value the responses of others and to be accountable to the group.
9. Students are reminded to thank their partners and return to their places.
10. Students reflect on the strategy and consider how talking to others stretched their thinking.
11. If appropriate, a whole-class discussion can be had on the connections between the prompts in all four corners.
12. The strategy is connected to the learning goal. Students are asked these questions:
    - How did this strategy help us learn…?
    - How does what we are doing today connect to the success criteria?
    - What was the most important idea in this activity for you? Why?
    - What learning skills or habits of mind did you use?
13. Students track their reflections in a learning journal, journal, diary etc.
14. The prompts are kept up for the learning cycle and are returned to if they can contribute to the learning over time.

Assessment Opportunities

- There are many opportunities here to listen for learning, to probe thinking, to extend understanding, to ask for evidence, etc.
- You will notice that the debrief of this strategy supports metacognition and self-assessment. It also asks students to document their learning. This is key to the development of self-efficacy and provides feedback for teachers and students.

Extensions

A popular alternative to this approach is to use a series of statements and have students move to the corner that most reflects their level of agreement. The four corners are labeled *Strongly Agree*, *Agree*, *Disagree*, and *Strongly Disagree*. The statements could be related to content knowledge or they could be big ideas from the course that you would like students to reflect on, select, and defend as a position/belief. They could be drawn from current events or themes in a text. This strategy can be really wide open and flexible.

Payoff

Students are actively involved, all voices are valued, mistakes/misconceptions are uncovered. In addition, both students and teachers have feedback related to the learning goals.

Strategy: Fishbowl

This is an opportunity for all students to participate either in listening in on a discussion or participating in a discussion. It can be used early in teaching students how to participate effectively in groups. They will practice listening, adding on, clarifying, questioning, etc.

1. Teacher selects a particular strategy or conversational protocol they would like students to practice. For example, students play with building on ideas and posing questions.
2. Students form two circles: a small one in the centre of no more than four participants, and everyone else in the class in the outer circle. Those on the inside are practicing a strategy: compass points (page 87), literature circle, three-step interview (page 84), etc. Those on the outside are observing and listening to the inner-circle conversation.

It is important to be clear about the roles played in both circles. Both are important.

Tips for Implementation

- Keep it light and playful the first few times. Have students pick from a series of topics that they are interested in talking about and that are appropriate for the classroom. Provide scaffolded prompts so they have a place to start. See Accountable Talk on page 63.
- Keep it short, perhaps 5 minutes in total for the first practice, and then rotate groups in.
- Outside-circle participants are practicing listening and collecting data about participation: Who contributed? How often did people contribute? Did participants make eye contact? Did people pause before responding, etc.?
- Provide both circles with a list of success criteria prior to the event and explain that this is practice to become skillful and self-aware group members.

Assessment Opportunities

As teachers, we can watch, model, participate, give immediate feedback, and engage everyone in the debrief. This is excellent preparation for more formal discussions and group work.

Extension

This strategy can lead to the creation of more than one fishbowl conversation happening concurrently, so that there are more opportunities for practice and self- and peer assessment. You can move from casual conversation to more-focused content-related discussion.

Payoff

- Opportunities for practice, feedback, and reflection in the moment.
- Progression toward becoming skillful communicators and critical thinkers.
- All voices are included and encouraged in this practice, and students build confidence and efficacy through deliberate practice.

Strategy: Three-Step Interview

This small-group strategy has specific roles built in: each student has an opportunity to be a speaker, an interviewer, and a recorder. The template on page 92 is an excellent way for students to record their learning and document the conversation. This strategy could be used before, during, or near the end of a learning cycle.

Think about where this strategy would be best suited for students to share their ideas, practice speaking, and capturing conversation accurately. It might be used as a check-in point for a unit of study and submitted to you to review and get a sense of where the students are, individually and as a group, in their understanding. It could be used for students to discuss a project they are working on and review progress to date. My students have used it to present a work in progress (e.g., an essay or any other writing task).

Interviewer: Ask the interviewee to share their work with you by describing their thinking and process, and by showing evidence of their learning. Your main purpose is to listen closely and to help them explain and clarify their ideas. It is most helpful to the interviewee if you pause and paraphrase. This gives them an opportunity to clarify and build on their thinking. You may also ask a question and/or ask them to support their thinking with evidence or proof.

Interviewee: Share the progress of your work up to this point. Highlight how you are moving toward the learning goal and share how you have met the success criteria. Provide evidence from your work. Ask the interviewer to provide feedback on your progress. What questions, suggestions, or next steps can they offer to help you move forward?

Recorder: Listen in and take notes on the template on page 92 to help everyone remember the conversation and to document their learning.

1. Students work in triads. Assign each student in a triad a letter A, B, or C, and then have them take on the role as indicated below:

   A — Interviewer
   B — Interviewee
   C — Recorder

2. The interviews can be formal or casual conversations about progress on a particular task or a review of content.
3. Each interview is recorded on the Three-Step Interview template on page 92. The box at the bottom is for summary notes from the interviews: pulling together observations, common challenges, questions.
4. After the first round rotate the roles.
5. Rotate the roles and repeat again, so each student has the opportunity to be a speaker, interviewer, and recorder.
6. Teachers might choose to collect and assess the forms for feedback, as they document student progress and learning at a particular point in the learning cycle. These are not for summative evaluation.

Assessment Opportunities

This is a great strategy to get a read of the whole class, in real time, and also to document where everyone is in their progress. You can use the information to form small groups for feedback and also to check in with individuals. You can pose questions on the template and have the groups revisit their conversations with another purpose related to the original aim. Again, this is a way of gathering evidence that involves observation, conversation, and a product. Students are active participants and you have an opportunity to check in with them during the learning.

Extension

This is a flexible strategy and can be used as a tool for peer assessment and feedback.

Payoff

Students are engaged in accountable talk, are active participants in meaning-making, and are supporting one another as learners. All of these skills are life skills and transferable to many contexts.

Strategy: Placemat

This is an excellent strategy to engage and capture student conversations. It can be used in many ways across the curriculum. Students work in groups of four, and each has their own space on chart paper. This space is used to record their individual thinking about a topic, question, prompt, reading, etc. This strategy can be used before introducing new content to activate prior knowledge. It is equally effective in the middle of a unit to process and engage with content, or at the end as a summary.

1. Teacher chooses a topic for students to discuss and organizes them into groups of four, either randomly or more intentionally, depending on the context. Each group might be working on the same question or there could be a variety of questions, one for each group.
2. Each group receives a sheet of chart paper and directions on drawing the placemat template; alternatively, copy and distribute the Placemat template on page 93. There is a space in the corners for each student and a central space for shared thinking that will come at the end.
3. Students to work individually in response to the prompt.
4. Using a round-robin approach, students share and build on each other's responses. Each student shares one idea at a time related to the topic. Students connect the ideas and add details to each other's ideas.
5. Once everyone has shared and contributed their individual ideas, the group organizes and summarizes their ideas into the most important points to share in the centre space. They need to assess the quality of their individual responses and select what is most pertinent and relevant to the prompt.
6. Teacher asks students to make sure everyone in the group is ready to share back to the whole class. This reminder will let them know that everyone is accountable to the community. There are many processes that can be used for sharing back: one group at a time, a gallery walk, one-stays-and-others-stray to hear group presentations.

This is an essential step, as it requires students to connect, synthesize, and prioritize what is most relevant and important to meet the demands of the task. If they miss this step, we will get a list of individual ideas rather than the deeper thinking, the analysis and synthesis we are looking for in their work.

Tips for Implementation

- All listening, speaking, and group norms are important to this task. Notice that Johnson's 5 (see page 77) are built into the task. Reminders about them can be very important, depending on how effectively students are working together.

Make decisions based on your students' strengths, their dispositions, and the quality of the relationships in your classroom.
- Timing can be tricky with this task, as some students will be quick to get going and others will need more time. You will know when to step in to check on progress as you are circulating and gathering assessment information. I often ask, "How much more time do you think you need as a group? Check in with each other and show me—5 minutes, 3 minutes, or 1 more minute?"

Assessment Opportunities

You will have opportunities to see and hear what students are creating and contributing. Depending on your purpose, you may focus on gathering information on a few individual students during this cooperative experience. You can choose to focus on the content and/or the process. Are students on topic? Do some students seem hesitant to start? Are there some resources students might need to get started: their notes, technology, or perhaps a little encouragement? As always, having a clear sense of the learning goal and the success criteria helps us and students remain focused in the learning.

Strategy: Suit Yourself

This strategy is adapted from The Collaborative for Academic, Social, and Emotional Learning(2022)

This is an excellent strategy to have students reflect on their experience in class or in a small group. It is offered as an optimistic closure, as they transition from one experience to the next or at the end of a learning period. They are also assigned to make these connections randomly, so they might feel a little stretched or vulnerable in making a different type of connection than they usually do. It connects head and heart to make meaning of learning.

1. Playing cards are randomly passed out to students.
2. Students write a reflection based on the suit of their card:

   Heart: something that touched your heart, meant something to you
   Spade: an idea/concept you want to dig deeper into and learn more about
   Club: something that helped you grow a new perspective, thought, or idea
   Diamond: a gem of wisdom you are taking from the day/class

   Students complete this first part of the task on their own, either on an electronic whiteboard or on index cards.
3. Students find their group by suit. All the Spades, Hearts, Clubs, or Diamonds get together and form triads or pairs to share their responses. Alternatively, to make groups of four—one from each suit—and take turns listening and sharing their responses.

Tips for Implementation

- Save this strategy until students know each other a little and feel comfortable connecting and sharing head and heart learning.
- Be flexible. If a student does not wish to share publicly, they can choose an alternative way to share their learning.

Assessment Opportunities

- This is an opportunity to gather data about cognitive and affective experiences in the class and what is sticking with students. It provides a range of information and allows for choice about what students choose to share. When students share publicly, it helps them learn about learning. We are all unique; what we remember and care about may be very different from others in the community.
- As teachers, we have the evidence of learning to guide our decisions, and students have had an opportunity to reflect on their experiences and learn from the experiences of others. This can be added to the learning journal or a digital diary.

Extension

This work might be extended to the learning wall or on an online collection of student learning. I used it to have my students read and respond to others' comments. They were asked to make a connection or pose a question on two other students' reflections. This contributes to building community and valuing different experiences.

Payoff

Students connect to the learning and to each other. We see that our experiences are all different and that our identities and experiences are filters for our responses. This can lead to another lesson in considering perspectives and noticing our own bias.

Strategy: Compass Points

This strategy is adapted from Project Zero's Thinking Routine Toolbox, Harvard Graduate School of Education (2022)

This strategy helps students consider the opportunities and pitfalls of an idea or proposition. It can be used independently and also in small groups. It can be useful partway through a unit of study when you are asking students to apply knowledge to a particular proposition or idea. It would work very well in a problem-based or inquiry project, a body of work, problems, ideas. Students can work independently and then collaboratively.

1. Invite students to do this strategy individually before engaging in the group; in this way, each student will come prepared to offer some ideas to the discussion.
2. Assign students to small groups and have them work through each point on the compass (see page 94 for template) — Worrisome, Stance/Suggestion for Moving Forward, Need to Know, Excited—sharing and consolidating their ideas and opinions. All the collaborative skills will come into play here. You might ask students to rotate leadership in terms of facilitation, note-making, managing time and materials, and monitoring group processing.
3. After all groups have developed a proposal or designed an approach, you might connect students in new groups using Four Corners (see page 81) for Worrisome, Need to Know, Stance, and Excited. This will allow for an exchange of ideas across groups. Then students can return to their initial group to share their discoveries and reconsider their responses.

Tips for Implementation

- It is possible to change the prompts to meet the particular context of the learning and discipline.
- You can have students do this individually to consider and evaluate information from a news article, a community proposal, a school decision, etc. Then bring them into groups to share their thinking and generate a group response.

Assessment Opportunities

- As students work either independently or in groups, we have an opportunity to see and listen to their thinking.
- We can ask students to submit their individual compass points as an exit ticket and post the shared thinking on the learning wall. Shared thinking can be both posted and explained to the whole class by each group.
- Students can document their learning and thinking in their learning journal, and reflect on their contribution to the group and what helped them to learn, i.e., a particular learning skill or habit of mind. Notice the development of both independence and interdependence here.

Extension

This strategy can be paired with a placemat activity and students can develop a shared response using the compass-point framework.

Payoff

Students apply their learning in a novel circumstance and also have the benefit of learning from and with others.

Strategy: Hexagonal Thinking

Hexagonal thinking is an excellent tool to engage students in making connections between and across ideas and concepts. You can use this strategy before, during, or near the end of a learning cycle, depending on your purpose. It can be used to activate prior knowledge, check for understanding, or extend and consolidate previous learning.

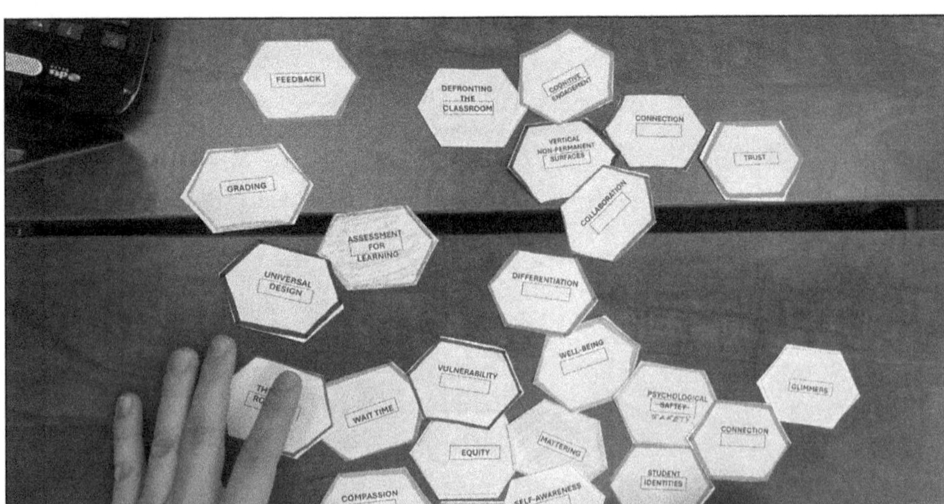

This can be done online or in person with each idea on a digital or paper hexagon. There are templates online to print or use digitally.

1. Teacher selects the big ideas or concepts of a unit of study and places each one on a hexagon. They can be framed as complete sentences or in just a few words that capture the idea. They could be visuals that represent the ideas.
2. Students work in small groups (no more than four) to discuss the best possible connections between the ideas. It is essential that the group follows all the protocols of listening, turn-taking, questioning, encouraging, etc.
3. There are many possible connections. The value is in the discussion and debate about why the ideas connect.
4. The sides do not all have to fit together. Some hexagons might connect on all sides and some might have only one or two connections. Each group's answer will be unique, as will their rationale.

Tips for Implementation

- Always review group norms.
- Select groups at random or partner students based on their strengths, needs, and interests. Remember that these groups are temporary and flexible, and that the more often students have opportunities to work with a variety of partners, the better able they will be to engage in peer assessment and build an authentic and active learning community.

Assessment Opportunities

- There are many opportunities here to observe and listen as students are working face-to-face. Remember that some of our best assessment information is gathered when we are listening to exchanges among students without intervening.
- If you note a misconception, pose a question for the group to consider and then come back to see if they have cleared it up. If their thinking is muddy or they lack a resource, probe and/or offer a suggestion. The point here is not to do the thinking for the students, but to help them develop their sense of self-efficacy by responding to the feedback in the learning moment to change direction and deepen understanding.
- This is also an excellent strategy for documenting learning. When groups have completed the task, you can ask them to take a photograph of their completed web and put it in their learning journal. It is a great source for self- and peer assessment. Students can note an idea that a peer offered that they hadn't considered and explain how it helped them. As a self-assessment, students can reflect on their contributions to the group and what they learned from the experience, both about the content and the learning process.

Extensions

- Students can share their top two connections and explain them to the class. It is worthwhile to probe hexagons that have few connections and to hear from other groups with different ideas.
- This strategy can be used across the curriculum to connect concepts and teach critical thinking. It is easily applied in Language Arts, Science, Social Science, the Arts, etc.

Payoff

This strategy allows opportunities for students to practice the following thinking moves:

- elaborating and clarifying
- building on and/or challenging others' contributions
- synthesizing ideas and creating new ideas

This strategy is adapted from Circles of Action, Harvard Graduate School of Education (2022)

Learning Journal: Circles of Action

Take a few moments to review the content of the chapter and consider how you might use and share your learning with others and in what context.

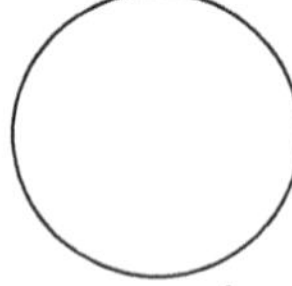

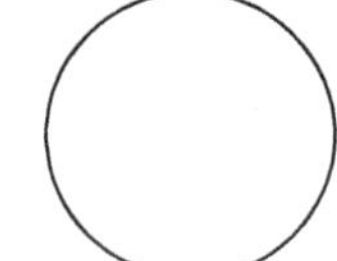

In your own classroom — With colleagues — With families and community

Muddiest Point

What is most unclear in all of these strategies and approaches to diagnostic and formative assessment? How might you seek clarification?

Habits of Mind

Habits of Mind

Managing Impulsivity

Thinking Flexibly

Striving for Accuracy

Taking Responsible Risks

Remaining Open to Continuous Learning

Responding with Wonderment & Awe

Applying Past Knowledge to New Situations

Persisting

Thinking & Communicating with Clarity & Precision

Finding Humour

Thinking Interdependently

Thinking About Your Thinking

Questioning & Posing Problems

Listening with Empathy & Understanding

Gathering Data Through Senses

Creating Imagining Innovating

Three-Step Interview

Interview 1

A — Interviewer: ____________________

B — Interviewee: ____________________

C — Recorder: ____________________

Interview 2

A— Interviewee: ____________________

B — Recorder: ____________________

C — Interviewer: ____________________

Interview 3

A — Recorder: ____________________

B — Interviewer: ____________________

C — Interviewee: ____________________

Pembroke Publishers ©2024 *Assessment in Action* by Theresa Meikle ISBN 978-1-55138-370-5

Placemat

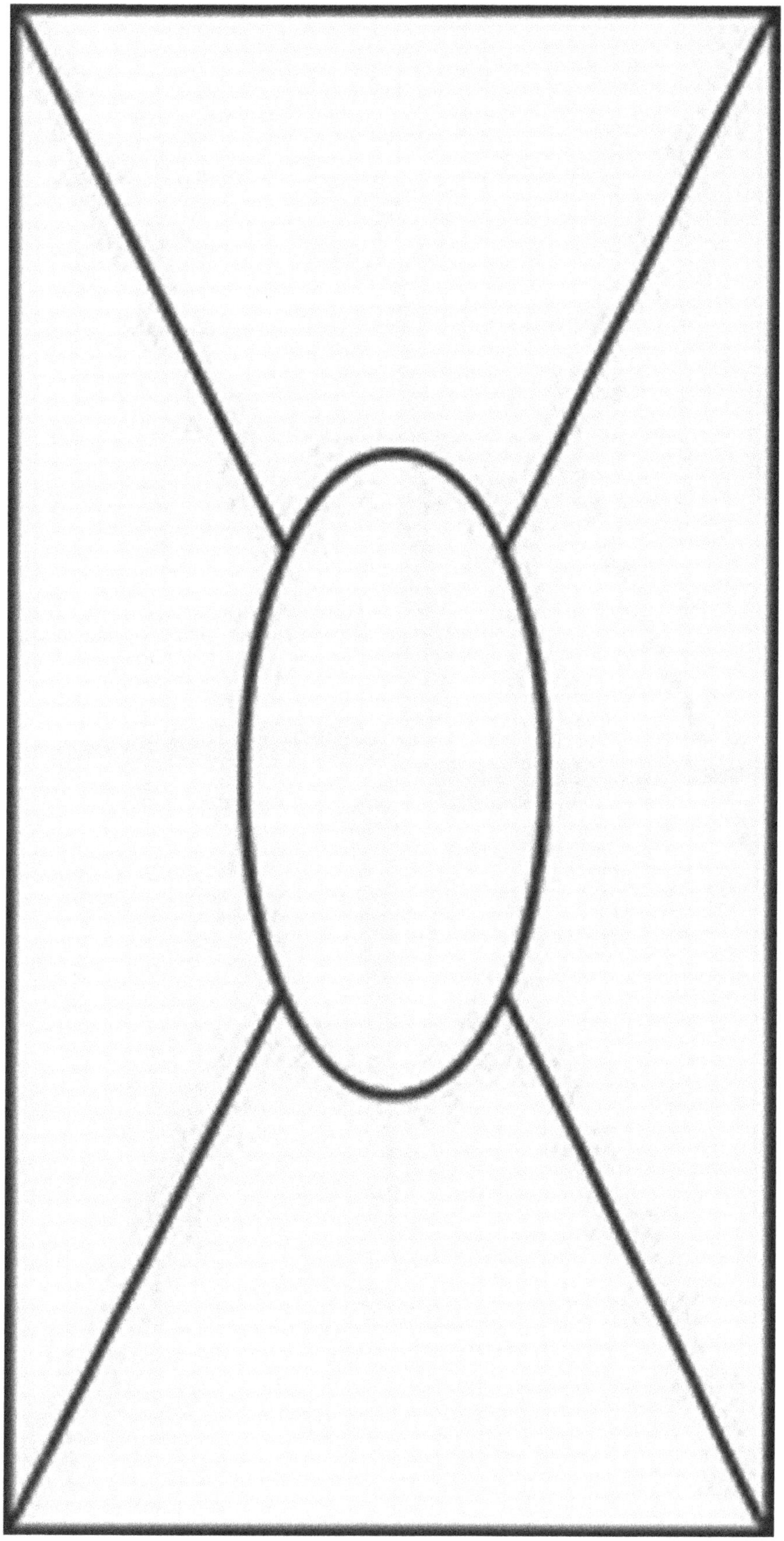

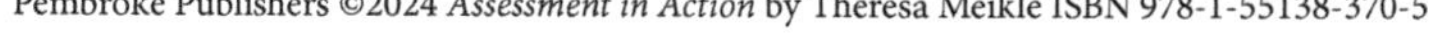

Compass Points

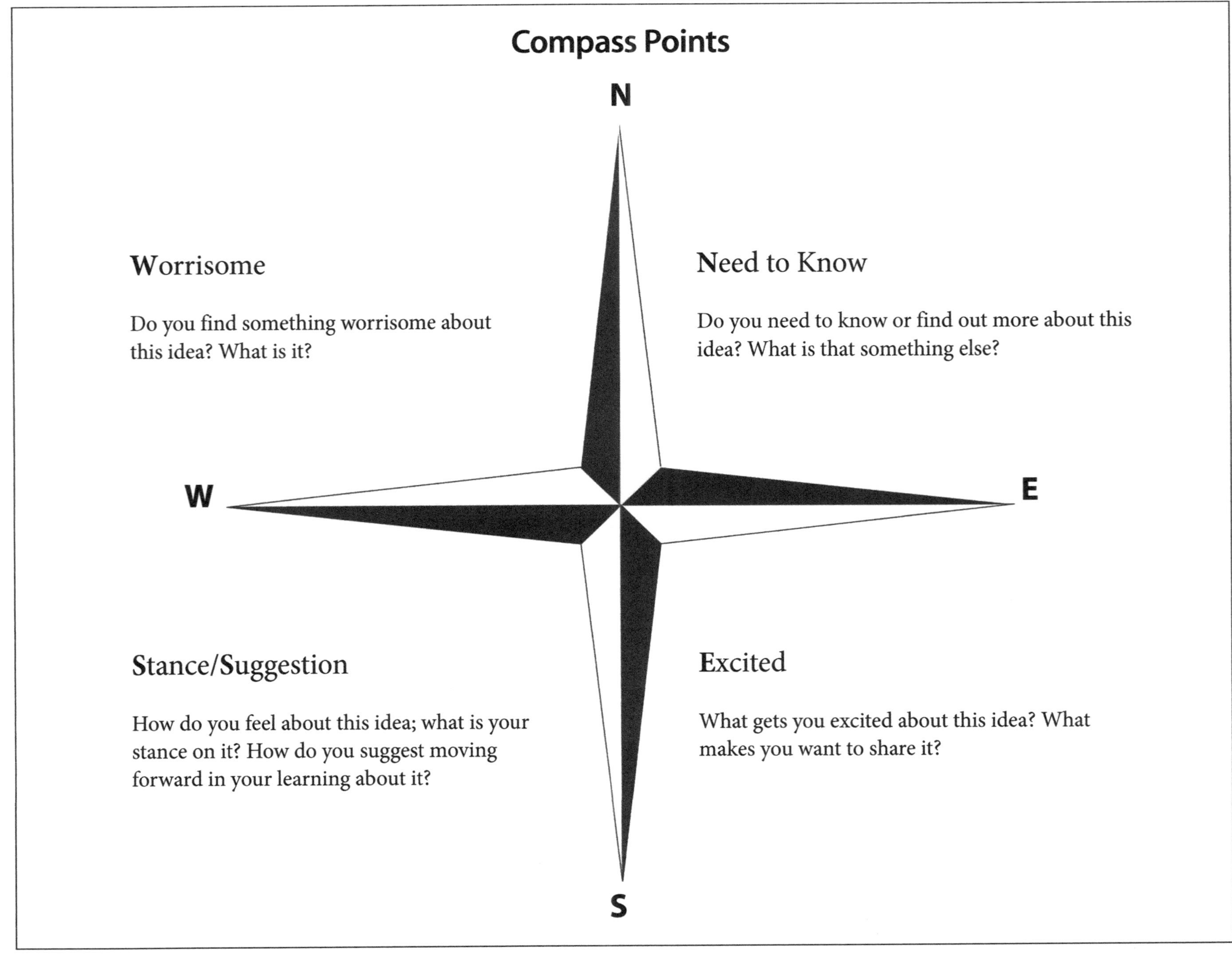

Worrisome

Do you find something worrisome about this idea? What is it?

Need to Know

Do you need to know or find out more about this idea? What is that something else?

Stance/Suggestion

How do you feel about this idea; what is your stance on it? How do you suggest moving forward in your learning about it?

Excited

What gets you excited about this idea? What makes you want to share it?

Pembroke Publishers ©2024 *Assessment in Action* by Theresa Meikle ISBN 978-1-55138-370-5

CHAPTER 7

Assessment As Learning: Self-Monitoring, Revising, and Intentional Practice

Prompt for Reflection

"Assessment *FOR* learning is about helping students become conscious of their learning moves and how to change them to improve their learning. Neuroscience supports this idea. The brain has what is called the 'progress principle.' That is, we will persevere and hang in there when doing hard things if we see progress... Just the act of seeing this progress raises the dopamine level in your brain's reward center. Dopamine is the 'yummiest' brain chemical, and we will keep doing the things that stimulate it. It's the brain's way of saying, 'keep going.' The degree to which we can get teachers to understand the connection between formative assessment and student agency, the more we will see students taking initiative in their own learning with eagerness."

— Zaretta Hammond in Knight (2018)

Can you recall an experience like this from your own life? Identify a moment when you felt empowered and motivated as you saw some progress toward a goal. Perhaps you have noticed that some of your students will persist when they meet challenge, others might give up and even resist. What are some formative assessment strategies you have used or might try to increase the likelihood of persistence?

Essential Questions

- How do we help students develop independence and self-efficacy?
- How do the practices of self- and peer assessment enhance motivation and clarity about what quality looks like?

Ultimately we are in the business of helping students become their own best teachers and assessors. The skills of goal-setting, planning, monitoring, and self-regulating toward achievement are lifelong learning skills and habits. So far we have focused on creating an interdependent classroom climate in which everyone plays an active part in the community of learners. We have been explicit about teaching both content and the development of skills to interact meaningfully with content; we are engaging students in meaning-making and applying knowledge and understanding in familiar and new contexts. We are stretching our learners and helping them see that their efforts matter. And, hopefully, we are shifting an orientation from one focused on grades to one that is focused on learning. Students come to understand that the tasks they are involved in are a means to the learning rather than something they have to get through or "perform."

Peer and Self-Assessment

In this chapter we will focus on self- and peer assessment. When implemented effectively, both these practices have a powerful impact on student learning. It is important to note here that these are formative practices, assessment *for* learning and *as* learning. Students are helping each other learn and improve during the learning; their work is not graded. Self- and peer assessment include the strategies identified by Wiliam & Leahy (2015) as activating students as learning resources for one another and as owners of their own learning. It involves students in accepting responsibility for their learning and investing in the learning of others.

You might already include these strategies in your classroom and find some benefits and some challenges. I have experienced both, in elementary and high school, and with adult learners. Taking responsibility for our own learning and acting on feedback from others or ourselves can be difficult; we encounter resistance, even from ourselves. So here we will identify some challenges to implementation and offer some suggestions and practical protocols to help students position themselves as active participants in learning.

Frey, Hattie, and Fisher (2018) use the term "assessment capable visible learners" to describe students who can use information to monitor their learning and to self-regulate. These learners have internalized the strategies that help them improve continuously; they

- know where they are going
- know what success looks like
- employ learning skills and habits of mind skillfully
- seek out and use feedback from others
- monitor, assess, and adjust their approach
- try out different approaches and see mistakes as opportunities to learn

We can support students in the development of these characteristics through engaging in self- and peer assessment. But we might meet with some resistance.

Take a few moments to consider your current beliefs about the value and reliability of self- and peer assessment. Complete this anticipation guide before reading the remainder of the chapter.

Teacher Strategy: Anticipation Guide

Before you read the rest of the chapter: Read each of the statements below and indicate your level of agreement by circling the response.

As you read: You might add to your understanding of assessment for learning and may revise your thinking based on what is offered here.

After you read: Come back and reread these statements. Circle your response in the *After Reading* column. Make a note of any information or ideas that changed your opinion.

Before Reading	Statements	After Reading
Strongly Agree Agree Disagree Strongly Disagree	External feedback, from teachers and peers, is more effective for improving performance than internal feedback (metacognitive processes of goal-setting, monitoring, and self-assessment)	Strongly Agree Agree Disagree Strongly Disagree
Strongly Agree Agree Disagree Strongly Disagree	Reliable self-assessment occurs as a result of regular practice with peer assessment.	Strongly Agree Agree Disagree Strongly Disagree
Strongly Agree Agree Disagree Strongly Disagree	Peer assessment is easy to implement and always welcomed and helpful.	Strongly Agree Agree Disagree Strongly Disagree
Strongly Agree Agree Disagree Strongly Disagree	Feedback provided too long after an assessment is not as effective as feedback offered in the moment.	Strongly Agree Agree Disagree Strongly Disagree
Strongly Agree Agree Disagree Strongly Disagree	Visible thinking processes and cooperative learning strategies are essential to gathering and responding to student learning in a timely way.	Strongly Agree Agree Disagree Strongly Disagree

Strategy: Anticipation Guide

Students connect their prior knowledge about the upcoming topic, issue, or reading before delving in. This helps them connect the new to the known. The anticipation guide statements help preview the topic and support students in reading, speaking, and listening more purposefully.

Tips for Implementation

- See Anticipation Guide above. Create statements for your students that are open-ended, rather than right or wrong. This will help students see nuance and other perspectives, and be able to either confirm or disconfirm as they read.
- This strategy can be used in pairs or small discussion groups before reading, listening to, or viewing a text. It helps students consider other ideas and to understand why they are reading, listening, and viewing.

- You can pair this with mini-whiteboards (see page 67) and have groups share their answers with the whole class, before moving into the learning and then again after the learning. This can be very effective in stimulating discussion and participation.
- Debriefing the responses as a whole class is very effective and helps you clear up misconceptions, clarify responses, and respond to emerging questions.
- This strategy is a purposeful scaffold to increase comprehension and to provide just-in-time feedback.

Peer Assessment

Engaging students in examining student work together helps them develop clarity about success criteria and tease out what constitutes quality. It is essential that they understand the learning goals, know what success looks like, and can articulate what is present and what is missing from a piece of work. In order for this process to be effective there are certain foundational steps that must be in place.

Teachers initially model peer assessment by engaging the whole class in discussion about anonymous student work. If you have already done this to help students engage in co-constructing criteria (see page 49), they are well on their way to being able to assess work reliably.

Connecting to Criteria

An effective process is to project the work and have students identify what has been done well; i.e., have them connect to criteria.

1. You can share the marker with students as they come forward to highlight the "best bits" or "interesting parts" or "juicy words." At this point, also ask them to explain their thinking: *What makes that part effective? What success criteria does this meet?*
2. After identifying what is strong in the work, move to the questions *What would make this work stronger?* and/or *Looking at the success criteria, what is missing here?* It is important to point out that we are always respectful in the discussion of student work. We are all learners and this is an opportunity for all of us to think about what makes work effective and strong. We are all learning to become more precise and to strive for accuracy. This reinforces the importance of reflection and growth.
3. Finally, have students turn to talk about what would help improve this work. As a group, generate suggestions for next steps.

Having participated in this process, students see what is expected of them in a peer-assessment protocol.

1. Read the work with an eye to connecting to the success criteria.
2. Draw attention to what has been done well.
3. Note what is missing or what could be improved.
4. Make a suggestion or ask a question to prompt the creator of the work to revise, review, reconsider.

This can be powerful learning if the following conditions are in place:

- process is clear and students have a checklist or protocol to follow
- students understand this is not about "grading" others' work
- students feel safe enough to share their work and trust their peers

- students are respectful and care for one another (this might mean that teachers are strategic in putting partners together based on the grade, context, climate, etc.)
- students see each other as co-learners who want to help each other get on an upward spiral (see page 74)
- students invest their attention in the work and in their peers
- cooperation is valued over competition
- students see that they are learning to improve their own work by assessing the work of others and connecting to the criteria
- conversations are encouraging, positive, useful, detailed
- feedback is clear, actionable, relevant
- teacher is actively monitoring conversations
- students receive feedback on their feedback
- students have an opportunity to use the feedback
- the process is debriefed as a class and reflected on in a learning journal
- adjustments are made for next time
- a teacher might invite anonymous feedback of the process as well (If the process is new to students, there might be high levels of discomfort or pushback. It is important for us to know how students feel.)

Implementing Connecting to Criteria

Helping students and guardians understand and value peer assessment can take some time. Being transparent with all involved is important. Some students might feel anxious about others looking at their work and some guardians might believe their child is being judged or criticized by others. Communicating with students and families about the importance of social learning and having them understand the value of student involvement in assessment and instructional process will be beneficial.

Be aware of bias in peer assessments. Some students might feel deep loyalty to their friends and therefore be afraid to identify any areas for improvement; other students might dislike someone in class and make hurtful comments. As Ruth Sutton (1991) states, assessment is "an exercise in human communication." It is essential that we build respectful and compassionate cultures in which all students matter and are valued. You will know whether or not it is safe for students to work together as assessment partners and provide the appropriate support in challenging circumstances.

Peer assessment can also be challenging because some students are less invested in the process than others. They might resist peer assessment and self-assessment because they want the teacher to do the thinking for them. They might want to check every step with the teacher before trying something. As a high-school teacher, I redirected many students to focus on providing effective feedback to their peers and to engage in meaningful self-assessment, rather than to depend on me as the sole authority on quality work. This is important if students are to accept responsibility for their learning. Sometimes students feel that teachers are the only ones whose feedback matters, but if we want to help them see that they are the ones who will ultimately manage their own learning, it is worthwhile cultivating a community of learners. In *Uncommon Sense Teaching: Practical Insights in Brain Science to Help Students Learn,* the authors state, "Remember, teaching is ultimately about what we get out of students' heads, not what we try to put in." (Oakley, Rogowsky, and Sejnowski, 2021, p. 98)

Receiving external feedback from peers and teachers is important and helpful; however, learning to give ourselves valuable feedback is beneficial and an important, transferable life skill. Students need to understand their own goals and monitor their own progress independently if they are truly developing agency and self-efficacy.

As always, time constraints often interfere with our focus on assessment, but if we make the time for students to become more proficient and independent, their learning is deeper and the quality improves. Another challenge that can arise is students who are not prepared with work to share with their peers in the time set aside for peer assessment. There is no doubt that this will happen; students will be at different stages in their progress. You can respond to this by making choices about how to group students. If students are still at a very early stage in a writing process, group them for a mini-lesson, a group feedback session, and then independent work. Others could be well on their way and need only a quick little conversation with a peer. This is the complexity of teaching. Having a flexible plan and flexible space for students to engage in their work as peer-assessors is vital.

Peer-Assessment Timed Protocol

Adapted from Wiliam and Leahy (2015)
35 Minutes (time can be adjusted)

This protocol can be adjusted by the context, grade, task, etc. Time and amount of detail expected in the assessment conversation are the features that will require adaptation.

2 minutes

1. Pairs of students exchange their work with one another. Depending on the complexity of the task, students might also have a detailed assessment tool—a checklist, rubric, etc.—that describes quality in student-friendly terms. (This would be something that has already been shared with the class and students understand. In addition, students will be more successful if they have already had opportunities to discuss work samples as described above.)

5 minutes

2. Reading Time: Provide sufficient time to read through the work.

3 minutes

3. Thinking Time: Provide time for each peer to look at the work through the lens of the assessment tool.

5 minutes

4. Question and Clarification Time: Students take turns asking questions for clarification about the work.

5 minutes

5. Planning Feedback: Students have time to note what is present and what is missing in the work. You can provide a framework like Stars and Stairs to keep this focused and manageable:

This strategy was developed by Jan Chappuis (2021) and is well use by many teachers to provide effective feedback.

Stars and Stairs

Stars provide specific, descriptive feedback about what is done well in a piece of work. Teachers tie the feedback directly to the success criteria of the task.

Stairs provide specific details about what a student has overlooked, has misunderstood, or needs to refine.

Teacher sample by Anna R.

	Descriptive Feedback:
STARS	★Great paragraph that is mostly all clear. Strong reasons and examples. Love your unique concluding sentence.
Stairs	For your reasons, remember to be clear and not ramble on. You're adding detail, but being very clear. Stay-on-topic.

5 minutes

10 minutes

6. Deliver and discuss feedback. Provide clarification as needed.
7. Apply feedback.

Noticing and Naming Strategies and Habits of Mind

See page 91 for a visual representation of the Habits of Mind.

As we bring students further along on the assessment journey, we are not only helping them acquire knowledge and apply their learning, we are also helping them build habits and learning skills. If you choose to explicitly teach learning strategies, it is important to have students notice and name them and to talk about how they are applying them in the learning context. As mentioned earlier, there are many ways to approach this work, and teaching all strategies could be daunting. Perhaps you decide as grade colleagues to focus on three or four strategies that your students can focus on and apply. Of course, all students are unique, and perhaps selecting one strategy you have determined through observation would help them will be your goal. As students learn the habits and skills and come to see how helpful they can be, they will apply them strategically. As everyone becomes more familiar with the strategies and uses them regularly, students can also provide feedback about them to their peers. Encouraging them to notice each others' use of strategies and learning skills will help them see their value and work toward their development.

Self-Assessment

It is best to involve students in self-assessment after they have had opportunities to learn about assessment for learning through direct instruction and involvement with learning goals and success criteria with their teacher and peers. They need opportunities to work with criteria and examples, and to have conversations about quality thinking and quality work. They need to be clear about the purposes of assessment for and as learning, especially that it is not for grading. They are not grading their work or anyone else's work. They are striving to produce quality work that meets the learning goals for the task. They are gathering information about what they have done well and what remains to be done. This is metacognition in action. When they look at what they have created, are they able to assess it reliably? Are they able to look at it as an opportunity for growth and reflection? Can they see what they produce as evidence of their learning, rather than something that requires their compliance, a hoop to jump through? Will they persist when they run into challenges, or will they procrastinate, get distracted, or simply tune out? As they become more proficient in understanding their role and responsibility as active agents in learning, they come to see the value of honest self-assessment.

Working with peers helps develop understanding of the learning goals and success criteria. Examining samples together and giving one another feedback helps students build a learning culture and the recognition that we are learning together; mistakes are prerequisite to learning. This is only true if, in fact, we catch our mistakes, identify where we have gone wrong, and redirect, based on our new understanding. External feedback, from teachers and peers, can have a powerful impact on this. Internal feedback, which comes as a result of monitoring, adjusting, goal-setting, and flexible thinking, helps students own the learning and work toward independence.

There are many tools available for self-assessment, both for assessing approaches to learning and to assess knowledge and understanding of content.

Students can assess their habits and learning strategies and use that information to adjust their approach to learning. Having students take stock of their development of learning skills, social-emotional competencies, and habits of mind supports them in developing self-regulation and celebrating their growth. Once they become familiar with the vocabulary and the success criteria of these transferable skills, they will develop proficiency in tracking their growth.

Learning Journal Prompts: Learning Skills and Habits of Mind

Prompts are provided on the template on page 105. They can be shared with students over time to help them track their learning, and their development of skills and habits that develop strategic learning processes and an increasing sense of agency. These prompts can be adjusted for any level from Kindergarten to Grade 12. You might choose to focus on teaching one habit or one skill at a time. There are many choices of how to implement and teach these skills:

- It might be of value to work with a colleague to plan to teach these skills explicitly.
- You might connect a particular skill or a few habits to a learning cycle or unit of study.
- Identifying these as learning goals alongside academic learning goals can be very advantageous, as students will see that process and content support one another.
- Use the images of the Habits of Mind (pages 122–125) as anchor charts to clarify what the habits look like in action. Have students use proof cards to show evidence of their use of the habits. This learning can be part of the ongoing development of a learning wall.

Learning Journal Prompts: Academic Learning Goals

The sample prompts on the template on page 106 can be adjusted to suit grade level, content, and context. Encourage students to point to specifics of the lesson and to add work samples as evidence. This is a simple way to track and reflect on learning on a regular basis and can serve as a resource for student-led conferencing.

Strategy: Reflections-on-Learning Survey

The Reflections-on-Learning Survey on page 107 is adapted from Wiliam & Leahy (2015)

Wiliam and Leahy (2015) suggest using a survey to gather information about how students are experiencing learning and how they are feeling in your class. You might choose to have students complete the survey on page 107 anonymously, so that you have a sense of the whole class. It will also provide you with honest responses of students' experience. As trust is built and the learning community is developing its own shape, it will be worthwhile to open up conversation about all of these learning and assessment feelings and interactions. If we are to support students to become both interdependent and independent, gathering and using this information to shape the learning will be invaluable.

Strategy: Collaboration Single-Point Rubric

The rubric is informed by the Habits of Mind identified by Costa and Kallick (2009).

The collaboration assessment tool on page 108 is a student-friendly way for students to learn and practice essential collaborative skills and habits of mind. It is a reminder of the collaborative learning goals and an easy self-assessment for students. It reminds students of the habits of mind that contribute to academic and social success. It can be used for whole-class, small-group, and partner assessments. Students can note what they are proud of and what they want to work on to improve. It can also be used to establish group goals.

Student sample: Grade 9 goal-setting based on previous strands of English document. Supplied by teacher Stacie O.

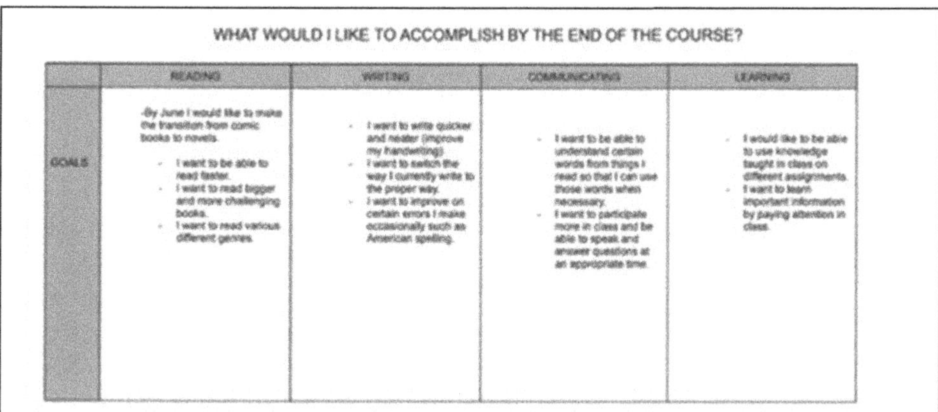

WHAT WOULD I LIKE TO ACCOMPLISH BY THE END OF THE COURSE?

	READING	WRITING	COMMUNICATING	LEARNING
GOALS	-By June I would like to make the transition from comic books to novels. - I want to be able to read faster. - I want to read bigger and more challenging books. - I want to read various different genres.	- I want to write quicker and neater (improve my handwriting). - I want to switch the way I currently write to the proper way. - I want to improve on certain errors I make occasionally such as American spelling.	- I want to be able to understand certain words from things I read so that I can use those words when necessary. - I want to participate more in class and be able to speak and answer questions at an appropriate time.	- I would like to be able to use knowledge taught in class on different assignments. - I want to learn important information by paying attention in class.

Strategy: Group Collaboration Tool

The template on page 109 is for older students, and can be modified, simplified, or expanded, based on where students are on their cooperative learning journey. It can be accompanied by feedback from peers and a whole-class assessment to consider their process. This is an often overlooked but essential part of effective cooperative learning.

Self-Assessment Strategy: Suspense Writing Anchor Chart

Hattie & Clarke (2019) suggest posting an anchor chart to help students use criteria to self-assess and improve their writing. It offers a summary of what students have been practicing in class and what is important to keep in mind as they are developing a piece. They suggest that these anchor charts can apply across the curriculum and help students understand and consolidate transferable skills.

This form of sharing and developing success criteria is more open-ended than "closed criteria," or success criteria that are more prescriptive. Closed criteria are related to specific, closed skills, "which have compulsory elements and usually need to be learnt or memorized" (Hattie & Clarke, 2019). Students will either meet the criteria or not. This is not a measurement of quality, but rather of a student's ability to remember and apply specific rules; for example, *start each sentence with a capital letter and end with a period.*

Sample Anchor Chart adapted from Hattie and Clarke (2019)

Success Criteria: What makes good writing?

1. What effects do you want your piece to have on the reader?
2. How will you bring about those effects? Adding dialogue? Including flashbacks? Incorporating descriptive and figurative language? Developing an event? Establishing a rich setting?
3. Have you avoided obvious cliched descriptions in your writing (e.g., *time flies, happily ever after, the night was dark and rainy*)?

4. Have you made your adjectives vivid?
5. Have you chosen interesting informative nouns and verbs (e.g., *the officer looked at the golden eagle* vs *the man looked at the bird*)?
6. Have you shown the reader how the characters feel and look, rather than merely telling them?
7. How do you want the readers to feel when they read the ending? Explore a few ways to bring about that feeling. Ask your friends and family for feedback. How did they feel when they heard the ending? Did their response surprise you? How might you use their feedback to revise your work?
8. Where might you add similes, metaphors, alliteration, onomatopoeia, or personification to add interest or depth?

The sample anchor chart supports students in focusing on specific elements of their writing during the writing process. You might select one of the questions and have students engage in peer assessment to give each other feedback in the midst of writer's workshop. As the writing is developing over time, examining mentor texts and co-constructing a rubric with students can help them understand and define quality. The rubric would be used to evaluate final products as a summative assessment. At this point students have had practice, feedback, opportunities for teacher, peer, and self-assessment. They have been on a learning journey and the final destination becomes clearer through the formative assessment process.

In our closing chapter, we will return to this idea of self-care/self-compassion and offer a few strategies to incorporate into our day for ourselves and our community.

Sample Anchor Chart adapted from Hattie and Clarke (2019)

Teacher Self-Assessment Tool

The tool on page 120 in the Appendix is provided for teacher reflection as a way of encouraging goal-setting and developing our own efficacy. The intention is to recognize our strengths, as well as areas for further learning or implementation. It is always helpful to work with colleagues to learn together and encourage one another to explore new approaches to teaching and learning. Like our students, we are cultivating habits of mind to refine and enhance our positive impact and contribution to our community.

Teacher Presence and Embodiment Self-Reflection Tool

The tool on page 121 in the Appendix can help us reflect on our own well-being and become more self-aware of our presence in the classroom. You will recall the importance of teacher self-awareness from page 15. Along with our students, we create the climate—the weather—of our classrooms and our schools. Taking the time to check in with ourselves regularly is very important, personally and professionally.

Learning Journal

Return to the Anticipation Guide on page 97 and review the statements.
After reading:

- Make a few notes or offer a few quotations from the chapter that might have altered your thinking.
- What might you try as a result of this learning?

Learning Journal Prompts: Learning Skills and Habits of Mind

Habits of Mind

Thinking About Your Thinking (Metacognition)	Persisting	Managing Impulsivity	Striving for Accuracy
Listening and Understanding with Empathy	Thinking Flexibly	Questioning and Posing Problems	Thinking Independently
Thinking and Communicating with Clarity and Precision	Applying Past Knowledge to New Situations	Gathering Data Through Your Senses	Creating, Imagining, and Innovating
Taking Responsible Risks	Finding Humor	Responding with Wonderment and Awe	Remaining Open to Continuous Learning

Learning Skills and Work Habits

What specific learning skills and habits are you developing?

Collaboration
Independence
Initiative
Interdependence
Responsibility
Self-Regulation

Prompts

Choose from the prompts to reflect on your participation and growth today. Remember you must always support your reflection with specific evidence. Explain how you used the habit or skill to help you contribute to your own learning and/or to the learning of others.

1. What habits of mind or learning skills helped you participate productively?
2. What habit or skill helped you when you felt stuck or lost? How did you use it?
3. As you worked in small groups or with a partner, what helped you stay on track or get back on track?
4. What habit of mind do you think would help you before you begin this project?
5. How do habits of mind help you when you are reading and/or writing? Which ones do you find most useful? Why?
6. What are your top three learning skills? How do you know?
7. What learning skill is really hard for you? Why? What is one thing you can do to improve?
8. How do you use these habits and skills outside of school: maybe in sports, in arts, at work, with other people?
9. How might these skills and habits help you in the playground or in the workplace?
10. What characters from fiction or people you know demonstrate these skills? What evidence can you offer to support your thinking?

Learning Journal Prompts: Academic Learning Goals

Select and respond to one of the following prompts related to today's lesson.

1. I was surprised to learn that...
2. I really enjoyed learning about... because...
3. I'm a bit confused about...
4. I understand...
5. A connection I can make to this lesson from another course/subject is...
6. I'm really interested in...
7. I used my prior knowledge of... to understand...

Reflections-on-Learning Survey

	Agree	Sometimes	Disagree
I believe that I can learn a lot.			
I learn a lot in class.			
My teacher believes I can learn a lot.			
I find it hard when other students look at my work.			
My peers help me learn.			
When I put in the effort, my work is better.			
My teacher helps me learn.			
I enjoy helping others learn.			
I learn more when I help others learn.			

Pembroke Publishers ©2024 *Assessment in Action* by Theresa Meikle ISBN 978-1-55138-370-5

Collaboration Single-Point Rubric

• I want to work on… • I will try to… • A habit of mind that could help is…	Collaboration Skills and Success Criteria	• I'm proud of… • I know this helped me learn because… • A habit of mind I'm getting better at is…
	• I paid attention to others. Managing Impulsivity Listening with Understanding and Empathy	
	• I added ideas. Thinking and Communicating with Clarity and Precision Applying Past Knowledge to New Situations	
	• I asked questions. Questioning and Posing Problems Striving for Accuracy	
	• I shared the pen, paper, space, and resources. Thinking Interdependently	
	• I spoke to my peers with kindness and curiosity. Gathering Data through All Your Senses Thinking Metacognitively	
	• I stayed on track, even when it was hard. Persisting Creating, Imagining, and Innovating	

Group Collaboration Tool

	All of the Time	Most of the Time	Sometimes
I understood my role in the group and accepted responsibility.			
I encouraged contributions from others by asking questions and building on their ideas.			
I listened with an attitude of curiosity rather than criticism.			
I came to the group with my individual contribution and preparation in hand.			
I managed internal and external distractions by setting aside work from other courses, accessing technology only to support learning and refocus my attention.			
Connecting to Criteria: Two things I contributed to the learning of the group: One thing I am going to improve on for next time: My next step will be to… Evidence of Learning: attach a digital or paper sample from your work for your learning journal.			

Pembroke Publishers ©2024 *Assessment in Action* by Theresa Meikle ISBN 978-1-55138-370-5

Final Thoughts

> "Like writing, teaching can be taught, mentored and made into principles; but its actual expression will always have an individual style, a personal approach, a unique coalescence of practices that cannot be replicated by others. In many ways then, the art of teaching develops naturally as a teacher allows experience. mistakes, and successes to form and reform their approach, and cannot be summarized easily."
> — Vitale (2021)

There Is No One Like You!

No one else will teach a lesson in exactly the same way that you do. We all have our own way of practicing both the art and the science of teaching and, in my experience, it is always evolving. How has your teaching and assessment practice changed over your career? How do you find ways to learn from and with others in the busy life of school?

Take a few moments to read reflections from teachers in the text box. As you read, consider how they have taken what they know to adjust their teaching practice to work with the learning context and the needs of their students. What evidence do you see here of

- assessment-for-and-as-learning practices?
- opportunities for feedback and metacognition?
- student as active participant?
- self-assessment and the development of student agency?
- teacher habits of mind that support student learning?

In the teacher reflections, you might notice the teacher habits of mind of thinking flexibly, striving for accuracy, listening with understanding and empathy, and being open to continuous learning.

Teacher Reflections

Sharing Learning Goals with Early Readers

by Aviva Dunsiger, Reading Specialist

Most of my students are still learning to read, so I need to reconsider how I share learning goals with them. When I taught Grades 1–6, I would often post these goals in writing—this written form is less useful, considering the students in my small group. This year I decided to start my lessons by briefly outlining the goals to students. This allows them to stay focused on our goals, as we are reading, writing, and communicating in different ways. I'm a big believer in voice and choice so, when possible, I like to incorporate some choices into this small-group time. Knowing the learning goals helps students think more about the choices they're making and how they will help them achieve these goals. We will then reflect on this work together at the end. Recording conversations with students throughout the process, and even listening back to some of these videos together, helps with this reflection. Students will note progress. We can also look back at learning from earlier in the school year, and students can compare their work now to their work then.

Assessment Is Messy

by Anna Rebello, Grade 3 Teacher

When I think of assessment in the classroom, I automatically see a process or journey of growth. As teachers, we know there are expectations, but the question is *How do we get those students through this journey to master these goals and capture them to where they have value to students and us as educators*? As educators, we are constantly capturing students' learning, whether we know it or not. It is not always in a beautiful checklist or rubric, but often it is in spontaneous conversations and observations. Those are the best kinds of assessment, I feel. They are organic, are in the moment, and often truly show how the student is learning. Learning targets and success criteria always need to be in place. Young children's understanding can never be measured directly. We must use a variety of tools and processes to ensure our assessment is not only reliable, but valid as well. If we are going to value the outcome of learning, we must also value the process of learning. This process can be messy. But it is so worth it for the success of our students.

Both these teachers, like many of us, are in the midst of the learning along with their students. They are bringing together curriculum and students through their presence and ongoing reflection related to the observations, conversations, and products their students generate. They are using what they gather from students as feedback to direct their next steps as teachers, and they are modifying their approach as necessary to support each of their students. This is the messiness of learning and teaching. There is no direct route to mastery.

We are always learning and adapting to the students in our classrooms, and learning from and with others can help us feel supported and valued in our school communities. This is not to say that we do not have challenging days and disappointing moments, but sharing our challenges and successes with others can bring us a strong feeling of connection, some laughter and joy in our own accomplishments, and the growth of our students.

This book is intended to be a support and resource you will return to regularly. There are many strategies available to us that can support student learning, but we don't need to do everything, and we don't need to do it alone. Perhaps you will connect with a few colleagues to try out a few strategies and refine them together to make them work for you. I hope you will see this as an opportunity to learn, practice, and create with colleagues and students.

Assessment Of Learning

Although the focus of this book is assessment-for-and-as-learning practices, I think it is valuable to share a few words on grading student achievement. We are finally called upon to use all of the evidence of learning we have gathered to report formally on student achievement. Whether this is reported as a letter, numerical, or written evaluation, it serves the same purpose: providing a snapshot of where the student is at a particular point in time. We want it to be a valid, reliable, and current reflection of student mastery of certain goals, at a certain moment. There are many considerations to keep in mind as we determine final grades. The following questions might help you make decisions about what the full range of evidence of learning reveals about a student's current achievement:

- Have I separated achievement of curriculum expectations from learning skills/behaviors/habits of mind/attendance?
- Have I paid particular attention to what is most recent and most consistent in the student demonstration of learning? Rather than averaging to produce a grade, have I considered which demonstration is most indicative of the student's current understanding?
- Have I reported on learning skills/habits of mind/attendance? Will students/guardians understand how these important attributes affect achievement and why they are recorded separately?

There are many considerations when it comes to determining a grade, and many resources available to support you in thinking about how to manage late submissions, missing work, group work, issues of plagiarism, etc. These are important conversations to have with colleagues and school administrators.

Ungrading

If our assessment-for-and-as-learning practices are supporting student growth, and students are given time to act on feedback, we are more likely to see that they are on an upward trajectory and making progress over time. This is the power of providing meaningful descriptive feedback without a grade. Hopefully the strategies offered in this book have supported students in their learning and the grades they receive reflect this learning journey.

I would like to share an approach that can help us rethink the whole issue of grading. Although most of our schools and institutions require that we submit final grades, many of the practices shared here support an *ungrading* approach to learning. Alfie Kohn summarizes the negative impacts of grading as follows:

- Grades tend to reduce students' motivation to focus on what they are learning; students are working for a mark, not to learn or explore ideas

- Students choose the easiest way to get the highest mark.
- Students focus on what is being evaluated/graded, not on what is to be learned.

Kohn (2011)

You, too, have seen evidence of students' anxiety and desperation around grades. Rather than focusing on learning and exploring ideas, some students become hampered by rubrics, marks, exemplars, etc., and look for formulas, short cuts, quick fixes. The rubrics and exemplars are not to be formulas or the one way of understanding quality. A rich understanding of quality comes through conversation, experimentation, inquiry, posing questions, feedback, etc. Learning is not memorizing and replicating. Unfortunately, I have seen many students make poor decisions in the pursuit of a higher grade—copying a friend's work, cheating on a test, skipping class for extra time to prepare. Greater emphasis on assessment for and as learning can remove much of this desperation and inauthenticity. If our classrooms are places of cooperation rather than competition, and if we are invested in our learning and contributing to the learning of our peers, we reduce the power of grades to dampen intrinsic motivation and curiosity to learn. We can enhance cognitive and social engagement in deep learning.

The following reflection from Secondary English teacher Stacie Oliver shows the power of implementing an ungrading approach in her classroom.

Ungrading

by Stacie Oliver, Secondary English Teacher

Shifting to an UNgraded classroom in 2021 has been the riskiest and most rewarding experiment of my career. Because the focus of UNgrading is learning for learning's sake, students come to see and accept "failure" as a necessary part of the learning process, something they cannot do when the prime motivation for learning is the extrinsic reward of a grade. In an UNgraded classroom, students feel safe to take risks, test their limits, and engage in deep and meaningful learning. They begin to value and seek out feedback, recognizing it for what it is—their own personal roadmap, a guide to help them get to where they want and need to be. UNgrading also helps students understand that the key to their success lies in the story of their learning, not the number on their page. This changes the classroom environment entirely to one of collaboration over competition, where students willingly both work with and learn from one another. And therein lies the magic of UNgrading. And what the journey should be all about. So plan the trip. Invite your students. Give them the map. Hand them the keys.

What do students have to say about a learning-and-assessment–focused classroom culture?

Student Sample: Semester Self-Assessment

Part 3: Story of "My Learning Journey" Story

The start of this semester vs now

At the start of this semester I came into the class with a little bit of writing knowledge and barely reading outside of class. I didn't have nearly the love for reading that I have now. At the start, I had a lot of mistakes in my writing and I didn't understand the setup I needed. I also didn't know how many drafts of one piece of writing there could be. I have taken the feedback I am getting and applied it to the next things of writing we get. This has really improved the way my work looks. I have also been reading outside of class a lot more. I read now whenever I get the chance to. I have started to speak in class a lot more. I have also applied that to outside of class now and started to make a lot of new friends as I've been talking to new people. This has led me to meet a lot of new people.

Student Sample: Group Novel Self-Assessment

U4: Group Novels

Task/Assessment	Literary Paragraph	BookTok
A. How do you feel about this piece? (strong, has potential, horrible, etc). Explain why. **B. How does this piece compare to the other ones you have done in this unit?** **Complete and turn in at the same time as you submit task to Classroom**	I loved writing this piece because it really felt like this was the ultimate test. After 5 months in the class this felt like the last big assignment and I used all the feedback I had got from previous assignments to create a paragraph better than all the rest.	This was the last assignment in this English class and I think I did really well. I was able to talk confidently and show clear examples of the big ideas in Darius the Great is not Okay. Overall a good piece but not as good as my literary paragraph.

You will make decisions about which of the principles and strategies in this book will support your students best. I trust that they will enhance your teaching experience while supporting your students in their flourishing, in realizing their potential, building relationships, and becoming contributors at school and beyond.

Appendix: Teacher Tools

- Assessment in Action at a Glance
- Unit Planning Strategies and Questions
- Three-Part Lesson Planner
- Lesson Planning Using Guiding Questions
- Teacher Self-Assessment Tool
- Teacher Presence and Embodiment Self-Assessment Tool
- Habits of Mind: Individual Images

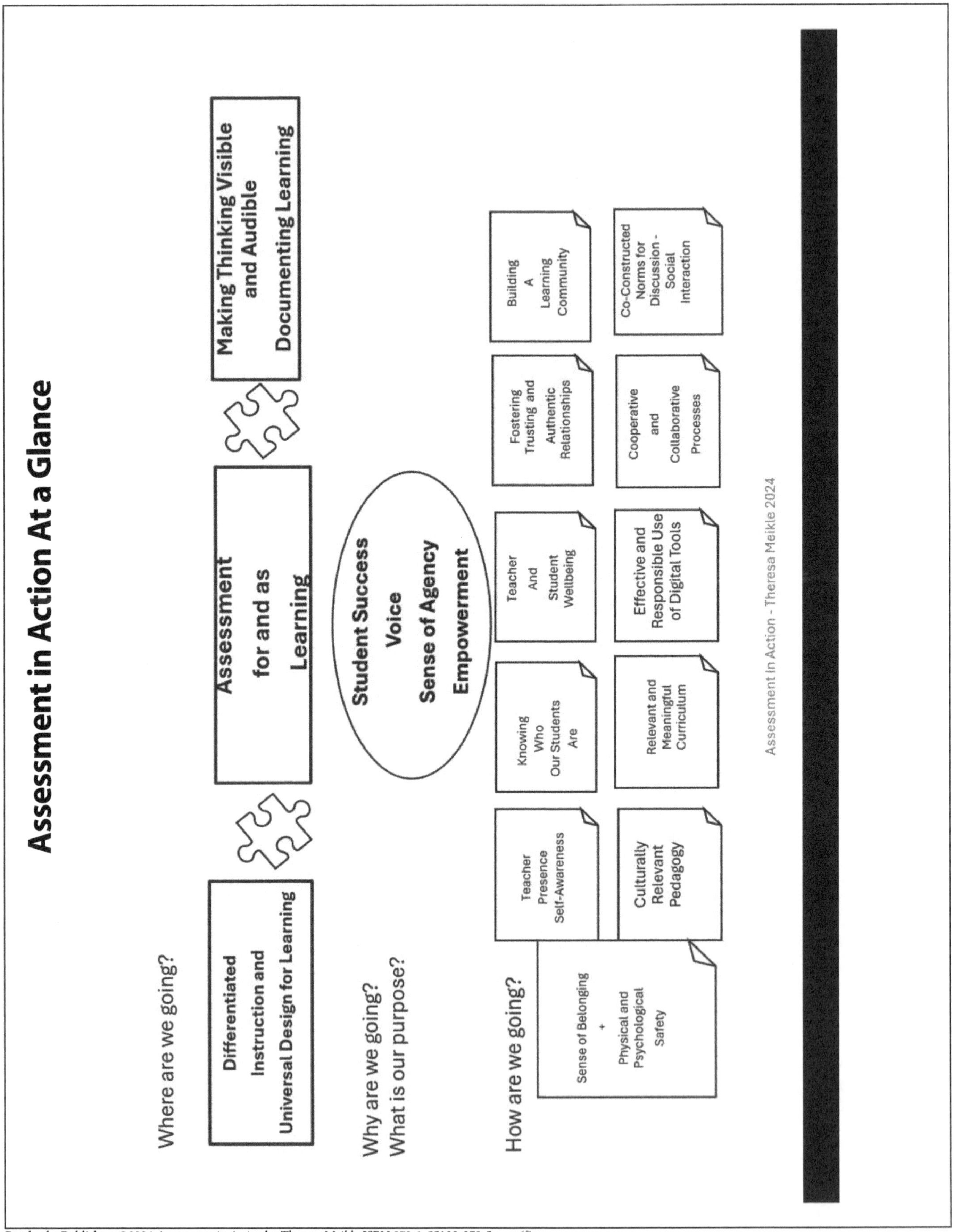

Assessment in Action At a Glance

Where are we going?

Differentiated Instruction and Universal Design for Learning

Assessment for and as Learning

Making Thinking Visible and Audible

Documenting Learning

Why are we going?
What is our purpose?

Student Success
Voice
Sense of Agency
Empowerment

How are we going?

Sense of Belonging + Physical and Psychological Safety

Teacher Presence Self-Awareness

Knowing Who Our Students Are

Teacher And Student Wellbeing

Fostering Trusting and Authentic Relationships

Building A Learning Community

Culturally Relevant Pedagogy

Relevant and Meaningful Curriculum

Effective and Responsible Use of Digital Tools

Cooperative and Collaborative Processes

Co-Constructed Norms for Discussion - Social Interaction

Assessment In Action - Theresa Meikle 2024

Unit Planning Strategies and Questions

Overarching Planning Questions

- What are the big ideas, either explicit or implicit, in your content standards?
- How might the big ideas in your focus subject intersect with the big ideas in other subjects you teach? Can you plan for cross-curricular learning experiences that engage students in relevant, authentic performance tasks? (Social Studies and Language, Science and Literacy, the Arts, etc.)
- How can you integrate social-emotional competencies, learning skills, habits of mind, and transferable skills into your planning? These skills and competencies enable and enhance academic achievement, transfer, and wellbeing.

Where am I going?
clarifying, understanding, and sharing learning intentions

Learning Goals

- What key knowledge will students acquire and use?
- What thinking skills will students develop and demonstrate?
- What key communication and application skills will students practice and utilize?

Assessment of Learning

- What culminating activity will anchor the unit?
- What are students working toward?

Success Criteria

- By what criteria will the learning be assessed?
- What exemplars will support students' understanding of the learning goal?

Where am I now?
engineering effective classroom discussions, tasks, and activities that elicit evidence of learning

Evidence of Learning

Diagnostic Assessment/ Assessment For Learning

- What prerequisite knowledge and skills will students require?
- What assessment and instructional tasks will provide this evidence?

Formative Assessment/ Assessment For Learning

- What evidence will reveal student progress, make learning and thinking visible, and show the full range of student understanding during the learning?
- What observations, conversations, and products will both develop and demonstrate student progress?

How can I close the gap?
providing feedback that moves learners forward and activating students as learning resources for one another

Formative Assessment/ Assessment For Learning

- Teacher Feedback/Peer Feedback

Formative Assessment: Assessment As Learning
activating students as owners of their own learning

- How will students be involved in the learning?
- How will students support one another in the learning?
- How will students self-monitor, document, self-assess, and adjust during the learning?
- What evidence (tasks and experiences) will reveal students' self-monitoring, reflection, and goal-setting?
- What requires revision, based on evidence of student learning during the unit and lesson (observations, conversations, and products)?

Three-Part Lesson Planner

Minds On: Opening the Lesson
Where are we now? Where are we going?]

- Inclusion/Connection Activity
- Review previous lesson and/or preview new lesson (information, resources, skills, vocabulary)

Hook: Provocation
- Capture attention
- Active participation
- Share the essential question(s)
- Share habits of mind/learning skills/social-emotional learning focus
- Share learning goal(s) if appropriate at this stage
- Share proposed agenda: activities/timing

Action: Diving Into Learning
How are we going?

- Connect to prior knowledge, previous lesson(s), relevant resources
- Engage students as learning partners/active agents in meaning-making
- Share exemplars and success criteria for work ahead
- Model/think-aloud as appropriate without doing the thinking for students
- Check for understanding throughout the lesson
- Employ strategies to make student learning audible and visible: graphic organizers, note-making templates, think partners, triads, thinking routines, etc.
- Chunk material and engage students in peer-self assessment throughout the lesson
- Build in retrieval practice: access resources, quick formative quiz, vertical non-permanent whiteboard work, review learning diaries, etc.
- Build in conversation and cooperative learning in order to reveal student thinking and respond accordingly
- Ask generative questions to support knowledge building and knowledge mobility
- Make explicit connections to big ideas of the course and transferable skills

Consolidation and Reflection: Closing the Lesson
Where are we now? Where to next?

Return to or reveal learning goals as appropriate
- What have we been learning today?
- What have we been doing to learn it?
- What is the evidence that we are making progress?

Self-Assessment
- What do you understand from today's lesson?
- What habit of mind or learning skill helped you?
- What is the evidence that you made progress?
- How does your learning today connect to your learning yesterday?
- What are you proud of today?
- What is unclear? Foggy? Confusing?
- What questions do you still have?
- Where to next? What is your next step?

Lesson Planning Using Guiding Questions

Minds On: Checking In and Getting Ready to Learn
How will I bring students into the lesson?
- start with a question, prompt, provocation
- activate experiences and connections to prior knowledge: quiz, questions, mini whiteboards, anticipation guides, digital whiteboards, carousel, think–pair–share, placemat, rapid writing, etc. (Diagnostic Assessment for Learning)
- address misconceptions
- share learning goals and/or inquiry questions as the lesson moves forward

Action: Making Meaning
How will students build knowledge and understanding?
Plan learning/assessment experiences so students move back and forth through collaborative, teacher-guided, and independent applications that develop growing understanding (deep vs. surface learning)

How will students interact with new content?
- paired reading, reciprocal teaching, mind-mapping, graphic organizers, thinking routines, discussion (teacher or student-led), four-corner conversations, line-ups, inside/outside circle

How might students be grouped as active participants and meaning-makers during the learning?
- random grouping, assigned roles, flexible grouping, assigned talk partners

How will thinking be made visible and audible during the learning?
- thinking routines: See, Think, Wonder: I used to think, Now I think; 4 Cs; Circle of Perspectives
- discussion groups: literature circles, Fishbowl, Circle of Voices, Three-Step Interview, Jigsaw

How will I differentiate in the midst of the lesson?
- assess student progress: formative assessment (for and as learning)
- just-in-time response to assessment information
- consider what is needed now, perhaps
- revisit a concept for the whole class
- group students for a quick conversation/redirection
- provide feedback and scaffolding
- sticky-note, question, reminder prompt, notice and name, criteria sample
- build in additional processing time and allow for extension
- review success criteria with exemplars; connect to criteria with students (small group or whole class)
- have students peer and/or self-assess and connect to criteria with evidence of their learning

Consolidation
How will I check to understand what students have learned?
- return to learning goals and/or inquiry question and success criteria
- allow opportunities for conversation: *What were we learning today?* vs. *What were we doing?*
- provide time for self-assessment: learning log, ticket out the door, connect to criteria, muddiest point, pose a question, 3-2-1 index card, digital diary

Teacher Self-Assessment Tool

	Most of the Time *I'm very comfortable with this practice.*	Regularly *I use this often, but I'd like to learn more/ refine my practice.*	Rarely *I'm not sure how to do this and/or why it matters.*
I share learning goals and success criteria with students.			
I involve students in co-creation of success criteria.			
I help students understand what quality work looks like through working with examples.			
I ensure students can connect success criteria to their work and the work of others.			
I have students use feedback to improve their work during class.			
I provide class time for peer and self-assessment.			
I engage students in assessment conversations during class time.			
I have students document and reflect on their learning.			
I teach learning skills and habits of mind alongside academic learning goals.			
I use student work as feedback about my instructional decisions.			
I encourage students to be instructional resources for one another.			

Teacher Presence and Embodiment Self-Assessment Tool

Teacher Presence and Embodiment	Most of the time	Often	Occasionally	I'm not sure	A question or comment I have about this prompt is…
I feel grounded and steady in my body when I'm teaching.					
I maintain a present-moment awareness while teaching and in conversation with students and colleagues.					
I am responsive to internal and external experiences while teaching.					
When challenging moments arise, I remain steady and alert. I teach from a place of connected groundedness.					
I convey patience, respect, and care while teaching.					
My instructional/ assessment decisions are grounded in ethical standards of practice: care, respect, trust, and integrity.					
I feel authentic in my teaching practice.					
I reflect on my practice.					
I seek out feedback from a variety of sources, and use it to inform my practice.					

Pembroke Publishers ©2024 *Assessment in Action* by Theresa Meikle ISBN 978-1-55138-370-5

Remaining Open to Continuous Learning

Responding with Wonderment & Awe

Applying Past Knowledge to New Situations

Persisting

THINKING & COMMUNICATING WITH CLARITY & PRECISION

FINDING HUMOUR

THINKING INTERDEPENDENTLY

THINKING ABOUT YOUR THINKING

Pembroke Publishers ©2024 *Assessment in Action* by Theresa Meikle ISBN 978-1-55138-370-5

QUESTIONING & POSING PROBLEMS

LISTENING WITH EMPATHY & UNDERSTANDING

GATHERING DATA THROUGH SENSES

CREATING IMAGINING INNOVATING

Pembroke Publishers ©2024 *Assessment in Action* by Theresa Meikle ISBN 978-1-55138-370-5

Professional Resources

References

Ambrose, S.A., Bridges, M.W., DiPietro, M., Lovett, M.C., Norman, M.K. (2010) *How Learning Works: 7 Research-Based Principles for Smart Teaching.* San Francisco, CA: Jossey-Bass.

Bennett, B., and Rolheiser, C. (2001) *Beyond Monet: The Artful Science of Instructional Integration.* Toronto. ON: Bookation.

Brown, B. (2015). *Daring Greatly: How the courage to be vulnerable transforms the way we live, love, parent, and lead.* Toronto, ON: Penguin Random House.

Buchanan-Rivera, E. (2022) *Identity Affirming Classrooms: Spaces that Center Humanity.* New York, NY: Routledge.

Carlsen (1991) – cited in Ritchhart, Ron (2023) *Cultures of Thinking In Action: 10 Mindsets to Transform our Teaching and Students' Learning.* San Francisco, CA: Jossey-Bass.

Chappuis, J. (2021) *Seven Strategies of Assessment for Learning 2nd Edition.* North York, ON: Pearson.

Chen, S. and McDunn, B.A. (2022) "Metacognition: History, measurements, and the role in early childhood development and education" *Learning and Motivation*, Volume 78, 101786. https://doi.org/10.1016/j.lmot.2022.101786

Clarke, S. (2005). *Formative Assessment in the Secondary Classroom.* London, UK: Hodder Murray.

Clarke, S. (2001). *Unlocking Formative Assessment: Practical Strategies for enhancing pupils' learning in the primary classroom.* London, UK: Hodder & Stoughton.

Clarke, S. (2008). *Active Learning Through Formative Assessment.* London, UK: Hodder Education.

The Collaborative for Academic, Social, and Emotional Learning (2022) Advancing Social and Emotional Learning Research, Practice and Policy. https://casel.org/events/advancing-social-and-emotional-learning-research-practice-and-policy-a-new-journal-for-the-field/

Costa, A.L., and Kallick, B. (2009) *Habits of Mind Across the Curriculum: Practical and Creative Strategies for Teachers.* Alexandria, VA: ASCD

Costa, A.L., and Kallick, B. (2008) *Learning and Leading with Habits of Mind: 16 Essential Characteristics for Success.* Alexandria, VA: ASCD.

Costa, A.L., and Kallick, B. (2009) *Habits of Mind Across The Curriculum: Practical and Creative Strategies for Teachers.* Alexandria, VA: ASCD.

Crane, R.S., Karunavira, and Griffith, G.M. (Eds.). (2021). *Essential Resources for Mindfulness Teachers, 1st ed.* New York, NY: Routledge. https://doi.org/10.4324/9780429317880

Davies, A. (2020) *Making Classroom Assessment Work, 4th Edition.* Courtenay, BC: Connect2Learning

Dweck, C.S. (2006) *Mindset: The new psychology of success.* Random House.

Earl, L. (2013) *Assessment as Learning: Using Classroom Assessment to Maximize Student Learning.* Thousand Oaks, CA: Corwin.

Flavell, J.H. (1979) "Metacognition and cognitive monitoring: A new area of cognitive-developmental inquiry." *American Psychologist, 34*(10), 906–911. https://doi.org/10.1037/0003-066X.34.10.906

Frey, N., Hattie J., and Fisher, D. (2018) *Developing Assessment-Capable Visible Learners, Grades K-12: Maximizing Skill, Will, and Thrill.* Thousand Oaks, CA: Corwin.

Friere, P. (2018) *The Pedagogy of the Oppressed.* New York, NY: Bloomsbury Academic.

Gregory, K., Cameron, C., and Davies, A. (2011) *Knowing What Counts: Self-Assessment and Goal-Setting 2nd ed.* Courtenay, BC: Building Connections Publishing.

Hammond, Z. (2015) *Culturally Responsive Teaching and the Brain: Promoting Authentic Engagement and Rigor Among Culturally and Linguistically Diverse Students.* Thousand Oaks, CA: Corwin Sage.

Hartman, H.J. (1998) "Metacognition in teaching and learning: An introduction." *Instructional Science*, vol. 26, no. 1/2, pp. 1–3. http://www.jstor.org/stable/23371261.

Harvard Graduate School of Education (2022) Circles of Action. https://pz.harvard.edu/sites/default/files/Circles%20of%20Action_2.pdf

Harvard Graduate School of Education (2022) Project Zero's Thinking Routine Toolbox. https://pz.harvard.edu/thinking-routines

Hattie, J. (2012) *Visible Learning for Teachers: Maximizing Impact on Learning* New York, NY: Routledge.

Hattie, J., and Clarke, S. (2019). *Visible Learning Feedback.* New York, NY: Routledge.

Hattie, J., and Timperley, H. (2007) *The Power of Feedback. Review of Educational Research, 77*(1), 81–112. https://doi.org/10.3102/003465430298487

Johnson, B. (2013) An Interview with Grant Wiggins: The Power of Backwards Design. Edutopia, George Lucas Educational Foundation https://www.edutopia.org/blog/interview-grant-wiggins-power-backwards-design-ben-johnson

Kanter R.M. (2004) *Confidence: How Winning Streaks and Losing Streaks Begin and End.* New York, NY: Crown Business.

Kohn, A. (2011) The Case Against Grades. Alexandria, VA: ASCD. https://ascd.org/el/articles/the-case-against-grades

Knight, J. (2018) An Interview with Zaretta Hammond https://www.instructionalcoaching.com/blog/an-interview-with-zaretta-hammond

Krechevsky, M., Mardell, B., Rivard, M., and Wilson, D. (2013) *Visible Learners: Promoting Reggio-Inspired Approaches in all Schools, 1st edition.* San Francisco, CA: Jossey-Bass.

Khokhar, R. (2021) 5 Key Ways to Build an Inclusive Learning Environment: A Reflection. rabiakhokhar.com

Kohn, A. (1999) *The Schools Our Children Deserve.* Boston, MA: Houghton Mifflin Harcourt.

Kohn, A. (2011) *The Case Against Grades.* Alexandria, VA: ASCD. https://ascd.org/el/articles/the-case-against-grades

Liljedahl, P. (2021) *Building Thinking Classrooms in Mathematics Grades K–12: 14 teaching practices for enhancing learning.* Thousand Oaks, CA: Corwin.

Markelz, A. (2016) *With-It Teachers Use ESP.* Alexandria, VA: ASCD.

Marzano. https://vtss-ric.vcu.edu/media/vtss-ric/documents/s2s-strand-2/2019-2020/Eight-Strategies-Robert-Marzano-and-John-Hattie-Agree-On.pdf – retrieved June 4, 2024

McTighe, J. (2018) *Three Key Questions on Measuring Learning.* Alexandria, VA: ASCD. https://www.ascd.org/el/articles/three-key-questions-on-measuring-learning

Morgan, N., and Saxton, J. (2006) *Asking Better Questions, 2nd Edition.* Markham, ON: Pembroke Publishers.

Muhammad, Gholdy (2023) *Unearthing Joy: A Guide to Culturally and Historically Responsive Curriculum and Instruction.* Markham, ON: Scholastic Professional.

Oakley, B., Rogowsky, B., and Sejnowski, T.J. (2021) *Uncommon Sense Teaching: Practical Insights in Brain Science to Help Students Learn.* New York, NY: TarcherPerigee.

Ontario (2023) Building a Stronger and More Inclusive Ontario: Ontario's Anti-Racism Strategic Plan https://www.ontario.ca/page/building-stronger-and-more-inclusive-ontario-ontarios-anti-racism-strategic-plan#section-6

Ontario (2010) Growing Success: Assessment, Evaluation, and Reporting in Ontario Schools. https://www.edu.gov.on.ca/eng/policyfunding/growsuccess.pdf

Ontario (2022) Learning for All: A guide to effective assessment and instruction for all students, kindergarten to Grade 12 https://www.ontario.ca/page/learning-all-guide-effective-assessment-and-instruction-all-students-kindergarten-grade-12

Ontario (2024) School Mental Health Ontario https://smho-smso.ca/

Ontario (2012) Third Teacher: Designing the Learning Evironment for Mathematics and Literacy K to 8. https://www.education-leadership-ontario.ca/application/files/1714/9884/6979/Third_Teacher-Designing_the_Learning_Environment_for_Mathematics_and_Literacy_K-12.pdf

Ontario Curriculum (2023) Elementary Languuage https://www.dcp.edu.gov.on.ca/en/curriculum/elementary-language

Ontario Curriculum (2023) Secondary English https://www.dcp.edu.gov.on.ca/en/curriculum/secondary-english/courses/enl1w

Ontario Ministry of Education (2012) *Adolescent Literacy Guide: A Professional Learning Resource for Literacy, Grades 7–12* .

Palmer, P.J. (2007) *The Courage to Teach: Exploring the Inner Landscape of a Teacher's Life, 2nd ed.* San Francisco, CA: Jossey-Bass.

Reinhart (2000) https://www.onted.ca/monographs/capacity-building-series/asking-effective-questions-in-math – retrieved June 4, 2024

Ritchhart, R. (2023) *Cultures of Thinking In Action: 10 Mindsets to Transform our Teaching and Students' Learning.* San Francisco, CA: Jossey-Bass.

Ritchhart, R. (2015) *Creating Cultures of Thinking: The 8 Forces we must Master to Truly Transform Our Schools.* San Francisco. CA: Jossey-Bass.

Rodgers, C., and Raider-Roth, M. (2006). "Presence in Teaching" in *Teachers and Teaching: Theory and Practice* 12 (3). https://www.tandfonline.com/doi/full/10.1080/13450600500467548

Safir, S., and Duganm, J. (2021) *Street Data: A Next-Generation Model for Equity, Pedagogy, and School Transformation.* Thousand Oaks, CA: Corwin

School Mental Health Ontario (2024) Identity-Affirming School Mental Health: A frame for reflection and action https://smho-smso.ca/about-us/identity-affirming/

Schu, J. (2022) *The Gift of Story: Exploring the Affective Side of the Reading Life.* New York, NY: Routledge.

Stiggins, R., and Chappuis, J. (2012) *An Introduction to Student-Involved Assessment for Learning* Boston, MA: Pearson.

Storeygard, Hamm, and Fosnot (2010) – cited in https://www.onted/monographs/capacity-building-series/asking-effective-questions-in-math – retrieved June 3, 2024

Sutton, R. (1991) *Assessment: A Framework for Teachers.* Oxfordshire, UK: Taylor & Francis.

Tomlinson, C.A. (1999) *The Differentiated Classroom: Responding to the Needs of All Learners.* Alexandria, VA: ASCD.

Vitale, K. (2021) The Art of Teaching. Yale Poorvu Center for Teaching and Learning. https://poorvucenter.yale.edu/ArtofTeaching

Vogler (2008) – cited in Ritchhart, R. (2023) *Cultures of Thinking In Action: 10 Mindsets to Transform our Teaching and Students' Learning.* San Francisco, CA: Jossey-Bass. .

Wagamese, R. (2016) *Embers: One Ojibway's Meditations.* Madeira Park, BC: Douglas & McIntyre.

West, L. Adding Talk to the Equation https://youtu.be/yhNcUQCu1w0?si=GbYT3oDU9OCOMp7

Wiggins, G.P., and McTighe, J. (1998). *Understanding by Design.* Alexandria, VA: ASCD.

Wiggins, G.P., and McTighe, J. (2005). *Understanding by Design, Expanded 2nd Edition.* Alexandria, VA: ASCD.

Wiliam, D., and Leahy, S. (2015) *Embedding Formative Assessment: Practical Techniques for K–12 Classrooms.* West Palm Beach, FL: Learning Sciences International.

Recommended Resources

Blum, S.D. (ed.) (2020) *Ungrading: Why Rating Students Undermines Learning (and What To Do Instead).* Morgantown, WV: West Virginia University Press.

Feldman, J. (2019) *Grading for Equity: What It Is, Why It Matters, and How It Can Transform Schools and Classrooms.* Thousand Oaks, CA: Corwin.

Hattie, J. (2023) *Visible Learning: The Sequel: A Synthesis of over 2,100 Meta-Analysis Relating to Achievement.* Milton Park, UK: Routledge.

Ritchhart, R., Church, M., and Morrison, K. (2011) *Making Thinking Visible: How to Promote Engagement, Understanding, and Independence for All Learners.* San Francisco, CA: Jossey-Bass

Schimmer, T. (2016) *Grading from the Inside Out: Bringing Accuracy to Student Assessment Through a Standards-Based Mindset.* Bloomington, IN: Solution Tree.

Stommel, J. (2023) *Undoing the Grade: Why We Grade and How To Stop.* Denver, CO: Hybrid Pedagogy.

Tishman, S., Perkins D.N., and Jay, E. (1995) *The Thinking Classroom: Learning and Teaching in a Culture of Thinking.* Boston, MA: Allyn and Bacon.

Index